WHEN THIS BLOODY
WAR IS OVER

HAPPY "TOMMIES" WEARING HUN HELMETS. 73.

OFFICIAL PHOTOGRAPH.
CROWN COPYRIGHT RESERVED.

Also by Max Arthur

The Manchester United Air Crash
Above All Courage
Northern Ireland Soldiers Talking
Men of the Red Beret
There shall be Wings: The RAF from 1918 to the Present
The Navy: 1939 to the Present Day

WHEN THIS BLOODY WAR IS OVER

Soldiers' Songs of the First World War

MAX ARTHUR

Introduction by Lyn Macdonald

PIATKUS

PIATKUS

First published in Great Britain in 2001 by Piatkus Books
This paperback edition published in 2008 by Piatkus Books

A CIP catalogue record for this book
is available from the British Library

ISBN 978-0-7499-2354-9

Designed and typeset by Sarah Theodosiou
Printed and bound in the UK by CPI Mackays, Chatham ME5 8TD

Papers used by Piatkus Books are natural, renewable and recyclable products,
made from wood grown in sustainable forests and certified in accordance
with the rules of the Forest Stewardship Council

Mixed Sources
Product group from well-managed
forests and other controlled sources
www.fsc.org Cert no. SGS-COC-004081
© 1996 Forest Stewardship Council

Piatkus Books
An imprint of
Little, Brown Book Group
100 Victoria Embankment
London EC4Y 0DY

An Hachette Livre UK Company
www.hachettelivre.co.uk

www.piatkus.co.uk

CONTENTS

All the hills and vales along
Earth is bursting into song,
And the singers are the chaps
Who are going to die perhaps...

Capt. Charles Hamilton Sorley, 7th Battalion The Suffolk Regiment, killed in the Battle of Loos, 13 October 1915, aged 20

THE SONG THE KETTLE IS SINGING (3).

Music has cheer'd brave Tommy lad,
  When he's march'd towards the fray;
Songs with a chorus make his heart feel glad,
  They drive dull care away;
But sometimes his thoughts fly back over the foam,
  And that's why he sings as he's dreaming of home.

AUTHOR'S PREFACE AND ACKNOWLEDGEMENTS

For the ordinary soldier, the First World War was an emotional and terrifying experience. It was a war in which thousands of men could die in a single day, machine-gunned, drowned in mud, gassed or blown to pieces. One of the ways soldiers coped was by singing, for singing raised their morale and for a while banished terror from their minds. They would sing as they came out after a tour of duty in the trenches, quietly at first, perhaps accompanied by a battered mouth organ. As the tensions of the previous days or weeks ebbed away, the singing would grow louder and bolder. Later as the *vin blanc* flowed in the *estaminets*, a riper range of song could be heard. At concert parties behind the lines or at the music halls at home, the singing went on with gusto. It was the soldiers' assertion of ordinary humanity in the face of extraordinary inhumanity.

A number of song books emerged during or shortly after the war. Although they recorded the songs, they seldom captured the actual (sometimes extremely bawdy!) words sung by the Tommies. In 1930, the *Daily Express* published *Songs that Won the War* (the soldiers probably wondered at the part they played!). A year later John Brophy and Eric Partridge, who had both served in the war, produced *The Long Trail*. Both these books were heavily bowdlerised and any vulgar word deleted. In 1978, EMI produced the song book of the film *Oh! What a Lovely War*, while *Mud, Songs and Blighty* by Colin Walsh had appeared in 1975, but neither had any background information on the songs. In 1990, Brian Murdoch, wrote *Fighting Songs and Warring*

Words, the first in-depth look at the songs of both wars. Roy Palmer's *What a Lovely War: From the Boer War to the Present Day* appeared in the same year.

What I have set out to do in this book is to gather songs from diverse sources and to give, wherever possible, the historical background to them, as well as the composer, and in the case of the parodies, the original words. As well as the songs sung by the Tommies, I have included songs sung by the troops who fought alongside them from Canada, Australia, New Zealand and America.

There are numerous variations to the songs, more than sixty for example for *'Mademoiselle from Armenteers'*, but I have tried to select an authentic example of each song as sung by the soldiers. Lack of space has, inevitably, led to the exclusion of many of the songs from the First War.

Many people have enhanced this book either through their expertise or straightforward help with collecting the songs. I would first of all like to thank Lyn Macdonald, one of the leading historians of the First War, for her excellent Introduction and for all the help and encouragement she gave throughout the compiling of this book. She offered sound advice and historical background to many of the songs. Sir Martin Gilbert very kindly read the manuscript at various points and gave me advice on the dates and background to some of the songs. Roy Palmer's book *What a Lovely War*, proved extremely helpful and I want to thank him for giving me advice on the manuscript, and correcting a number of errors. I would like to also thank: Sarah Theodosiou for her creativity in designing the book; Richard Pitkin of the *Illustrated London News* picture library, who supplied some of the pictures, in particular the Bruce Bairnsfather cartoons; *Punch* magazine, for the use of cartoons from their archives; Clive Smith of Memories for the First War postcards; Richard Golland, Head of Printed Books at the Imperial War Museum, and his first-rate staff; the National Army Museum were also most helpful; Tonie and Valmai Holt kindly sent me notes on a number of the songs; Carl Spadoni of the McMasters University, Hamilton, sent me an excellent selection of Canadian songsheets; Bob Bolton e-mailed me a number of Australian songs, and supplied details on their background; Gervase Webb sent me interesting notes on '*Tipperary*' as well as details on a number of other songs; Tom May generously sent me his lifetime's collection of First World War songs; Peter Vansittart, the author of *Voices from the Great War*, gave me background information on a number of songs. I was advised about the details and the component parts of the Royal Flying Corps aircraft by Don McClen. I would also like to thank EMI and Chappell's for their kind permission to publish a number of songs in this work; if I have failed to track down the copyright holder of a particular song, then I would like to extend my apologies. Ruth Cowen gave considerable support throughout. Finally I would like to thank my editor Alan Brooke for his sterling work and enthusiasm, as well as for his help with the illustrations.

I am grateful for the help from all sources; any errors that remain are entirely my responsibility.

INTRODUCTION

By Lyn Macdonald

It is a strange and inexplicable fact that the strains of '*Keep the Home Fires Burning*' induce a poignant sense of nostalgia in people born half a century or more after the First World War ended. But – especially when combined with the plaintive tones of a mouth organ – that melody automatically conjures up an image of weary Tommies in the trenches, just as a rousing rendering of '*Tipperary*' or '*Pack up Your Troubles*' evokes a mental picture of cheery Tommies on the march.

Clichés, to be sure, and perhaps the empathy they induce is also a cliché of a kind. Old Soldiers sang them as lustily as any at post–war reunions but although, with hindsight, such songs seem to epitomise the Great War, during the war itself they were associated far more closely with the Home Front. But the variety of music was boundless, ranging from those well-known commercially written war-songs, through music-hall choruses, popular songs from stage musicals and sentimental ballads, to the bawdy, ironic parodies that were current in the Army. Music loomed large in the First World War and, by its very diversity, still strongly reflects the spirit of its time.

And what a time it was! Until 1914 the British Empire was still ensconced on the high moral uplands of the Victorian age, girded by solid virtues, complacent in its certainty of its place in the world, with a God-given right if not to rule that world, at least to govern a significant part of it, spreading the light of its superior civilization to the far corners of the earth. The Victorian era did not die with the demise of the old Queen-Empress in 1901 at the birth of a new century: it began to skid to a halt in 1914 at the start of the Great War. By the time it ended, a new era and a new world had been born and the music of the First World War can be a pungent reminder that this was a society in transition.

The generation that fought it were Victorians to a man. Men of the Regular Army were even mid-Victorians – those legendary 'Soldiers of the Queen' who had served her in the furthest reaches of her Empire or fought at Omdurman or Spion Kop. Even the youngest of the adventurous youths who joined Kitchener's Army by the hundred thousand had been born while the Queen still occupied the throne and were nurtured and moulded by the long-accepted mores and disciplines of what was generally accepted as an age of enlightenment.

It was certainly an inventive age. In the lifetime of lads who joined the Army in 1914 at the age of 19 (or not infrequently younger) they had seen Bleriot fly across the English Channel, the birth of film as a popular entertainment, the development of the pneumatic tyre and the explosion of cycling as an everyday means of transport. A fortunate few even owned motor-bikes. People had become accustomed to the sight of motor-vehicles in the streets and aeroplanes in the sky. Wireless was emerging from its experimental infancy, telephones were no longer new-fangled devices, gramophones were commonplace for those who could afford them. Pianos could be purchased 'on the never never' for as little as a shilling a week, and every respectable household which aspired to an aspidistra in the window wanted a piano in the parlour. There was an upright piano in every church hall, every boys' club and in almost every saloon bar where the popular Saturday night sing-song could be enjoyed, even by the poorest, for the price of a ginger ale, sipped slowly to last the evening. There were thousands of accomplished pianists and many who could play by ear so, one way or another, in any gathering there was always someone who could strum out a tune on the piano.

But even the music was changing. Gramophone records were not expensive, sheet music could be bought for a few pence and ragtime, which had crossed the Atlantic a few years earlier, was still the rage. *'C'mon and hear, c'mon and hear, Alexander's ragtime band...'* Every messenger boy could whistle or warble it. *'C'mon along, c'mon along, It's the best band in the land, You can hear a bugle call like you never heard before, So natural that you wanna go to war...'*. By an odd irony it was not long before those words inspired one of the earliest of the many parodies of the war. *'C'mon and join, c'mon and join, c'mon and join Lord Kitchener's Army...'*.

The troops had much in common with the legendary preacher, the Rev. Rowland Hill, of whom it was said, 'He did not see any reason why the devil should have all the good tunes.' In the case of the Army the soldiers saw no reason why good hymn tunes should not serve equally well for less reverent purposes – especially those which required very little adaptation to suit the circumstances. So many men had accepted the invitation to *'c'mon and join Lord Kitchener's Army'* that, even with textile and armaments factories working flat out and round the clock, it was impossible either to kit them all out or arm them immediately. Tens of thousands of recruits who were still training in ignominious civvies and drilling with wooden 'rifles', long after they had expected to be marching to the front in heroic khaki, found that one familiar hymn fitted the bill: *There is a happy land, far, far away; Where saints in glory stand, bright, bright as day; O how they sweetly sing, Worthy is our Saviour King; Loud let his praises sing, Praise, praise for aye.* Every child could sing it, for it had a catchy tune and was a favourite Sunday school hymn, but now some impatient would-be-warriors hit on a better version:

> *Where are our uniforms?*
> *Far, far away.*
> *When will our rifles come?*
> *P'raps, p'raps some day.*
> *All we need is just a gun,*
> *Then we'll chase the bloody Hun.*
> *Think of us when we are gone,*
> *Far, far away.*

Most had been brought up to attend church regularly. The strictest families might attend church or chapel as often as three times on Sundays, most children were sent to Sunday school, and the older ones to Bible Class. Religious observance was a sign of that much-prized 'respectability' which was a hallmark of the disciplined Victorian age. There was religious instruction in schools, as well as morning prayers and hymn singing, and children were encouraged to join organisations affiliated to the churches. The Boy Scouts with their code of clean-living morality had strong religious overtones, though the uniform was not cheap and only boys of fairly well-off families could afford to join. Still, for the price of a pill-box hat and a belt, which cost only coppers, The Boys' Brigade and The Church Lads Brigade were open to all, and they too had their annual camps, their football teams, their sports, good company and jolly sing-songs in the Church Hall which always ended with a hymn and a prayer. The Band of Hope, one of many Temperance organisations, was also popular, for there were exciting lantern lectures luridly illustrating the evils of the demon drink, with free tea and buns and jolly hymn-singing at the end of the evening. '*Yield not to temptation, for yielding is sin/ Each victory will help you, some other to win*' trilled the inveterate young sinners to whom a glass of lemonade represented the height of dissipation, '*Shun evil companions, bad language eschew/ Look ever to Jesus, He will carry you through.*'

All in all, it made an enjoyable evening and, as with Sunday school, for those who qualified by 'regular atten-dance', there were the annual treats of the Summer Picnic and the Christmas Social. The Salvation Army with its oohm-pah-pah bands and even jollier hymn tunes provided free entertainment on the street corners of any sizeable town, and small boys would follow them for miles. It was hardly surprising that when some irreverent ditty required a tune, a so-familiar hymn tune came easily to mind – and if, at first, they struck the more strait-laced new arrivals as sacrilegious, it was seldom long before they were singing away as lustily as the rest. '*We are Fred Karno's army/ What bloody use are we...*' – (That was 'The Church's One Foundation is Jesus Christ our Lord'). '*When this bloody war is over/ Oh how happy I shall be/ When I get my civvy clothes on/ No more soldering for me...*' (That was, 'What a Friend we have in Jesus, all our sins and griefs to bear...') And, as the war went on, the lugubrious chant which more than any other summed up the universal mood of the resigned, but fed-up Tommy: '*Marching, marching, marching/ Always bloody well marching… Raining, raining, raining/ Always bloody well raining… Grousing, grousing, grousing/ Always bloody well grousing…'.* The variations were infinite, it could carry a company over miles of monotonous march, and the original ('Holy, Holy, Holy, Lord God Almighty') was not half so expressive. By the later stages of the war many soldiers were a little less inclined to reverence and a good deal more cynical. *'Onward Christian Soldiers, marching as to war/ With the Corps Commander, safely in the rear'.* That particular ditty was disapproved of by authority, even if some battalion officers had a sneaking sympathy with the half-jocular sentiment. But it was clearly not good for morale.

The Army laid great stress on morale and went to considerable lengths to keep it high. Regular leave was important and the passage of mail from home, through the Army Postal Service, was given the same precedence as the shipping of rations and ammunition. Parcels and letters from England sometimes arrived at the front two days after they were posted, although those from the north took just a little longer. After the first frantic months, when the war had 'settled down', Regimental bands which had stayed behind when the Army went to war, were sent out from Regimental Depots in Britain. But, as the war gained momentum and the Army grew, there were not nearly enough of them to go round. Later, when well-wishers were able to raise the substantial sum necessary for the purchase of instruments, and a Brigade (or even a Battalion) could find musicians in its ranks, new bands were even started in France with the blessing of the Army. One patriotic father, whose son was a Captain in the 5th Lancashire Fusiliers, even met the entire cost of a band for the battalion out of his own pocket. It cost a pretty penny, but he could well afford it for his name was Tickler, the manufacturer who supplied his famous – or infamous – jam to the entire Army, and Captain Tickler's men were doubtless of the opinion that he owed them a favour! The Captain remembered:

They were very cheeky! They came and said, Do you think we could have a band? The one we had was left behind! They'd got a catalogue and everything from Boosey and Hawkes. With the instruments marked on it, and all the extras too! So I wrote to Father and sent the catalogue and asked him. Less than a week later I got a wire from Father which said 'Bought band and it is on its way'. As quick as that! Well it came while we were out of the line. The first morning the men we'd picked to play went off and practised in woods somewhere, so that we wouldn't hear them until they were ready. Then we got going. We used to play for the whole Brigade and for parades when they were presenting decorations, and field days and so on – and, my word, what a difference it makes! It's lovely. It puts a swing into you. They did enjoy it, of course. They loved it! They used to swagger through villages and all the French and Belgian people came out to watch them. After Passchendaele it did a lot for the morale of the Battalion. Of course they knew where it had come from – and I don't know if they thought they'd got a bit of their own back for this eternal plum and apple jam they all complained about. Before the war we had no sale for apple mixtures unless there was a slump when people wanted something for fourpence. But the firm had to produce so much to supply the Army that there was no alternative.

The fame of the ubiquitous 'Plum and Apple' even reached the London stage in a musical play written by Bruce Bairnsfather. Arthur Bouchier played the part of his character 'Old Bill'. His rendering of *'Plum and Apple, apple and plum... We've all had some...'* drew roars of appreciation from the audience, particulary from soldiers on leave, and it was soon taken up, and sung even more feelingly, by the troops at the front. Though the men of the 5th Lancs. – or at least the men of Bill Tickler's company – in appreciation of their band, tactfully avoided singing in his hearing a more vulgar song favoured by the troops. It was sung by the 5th Lancs., unsurprisingly, to the tune of *'A Lassie from Lancashire'*. *'I've seen maggots in Tickler's jam/ filthy maggots in Ticker's jam/ I've seen maggots in Tickler's jam/ crawling round...'*

For obvious reasons, there was not much singing in the trenches where it was wise not to attract the attention of the enemy. But occasionally in quiet sectors, where the lines were close together and the night was clear and still, the sound of a mouth organ or voices singing would drift across No Man's Land to the trenches opposite. Eventually orders came from on high that absolute silence must be observed. German newspapers could be obtained by British Intelligence through neutral Switzerland, and one carried a fairly accurate translation of a song that was frequently heard rising from the British trenches: *'I want to go home, I want to go home/ I don't want to go in the trenches no more, where coalbox and whizz-bangs they whistle and roar/ Take me over the sea, where the Alleyman can't get at me/ Oh my! I don't want to die, I want to go home.'* The report came to the triumphant conclusion that the morale of the British Army was so low that the war was bound to end soon.

For the three years that were to elapse before it did, the morale of the British front line troops remained remarkably high, and despite the perils and discomfort of their stints in the trenches, and the weary monotony of labour in the hinterland, off-duty – even in a draughty barn – they contrived to enjoy themselves as best they could. There was usually an *estaminet* or a canteen hut within tramping distance, where there were warm surroundings, cheap beer and *vin blanc*, and if there was no piano to accompany the inevitable sing-song, it was often a simple matter to acquire one which, even if slightly battered could be patched up sufficiently to produce a tune. The back areas were so frequently shelled that (so the Tommies reasoned) it was not so much looting as 'rescuing' something which might easily be 'lost by enemy action'. Someone would pay for it in that almost never-never- land of 'After the War'. Officers turned an indulgent eye, though 'looting' was a punishable military offence, and even connived at it, since a piano was also a desirable addition to the Officers' Mess – and the Transport Officer could be relied on to find a place for it in the baggage train when they moved on. In any event, it was all good for morale.

One thing which could be guaranteed to uplift the spirit of the troops, and a highlight of rest periods behind the immediate front, was a visit to a concert party. They started in a small way, but eventually almost every Division had its own entertainment troupe – *The Diamonds* of the 29th Division (the Divisional insignia was diamond-shaped), *The Jocks* of the 15th (Scottish) Division, *The Balmorals* of the 51st, *The Anzac Coves* which was obviously Australian, *The Tykes* which plainly belonged to Yorkshire and *The Jesmond Jesters* to Tyneside. There were *The Pedlars, The Barn Owls,* and *The Follies*. There were *The Shrapnels, The Duds, The Tivolis*. The Canadians had *The Dumbbells*, and there were literally scores of others up and down the line. One of the most popular was *The Verey Lights*, whose fame spread far beyond the 20th Division. It was run by Captain Henson, Captain Gilbey and Bandmaster Eldridge of the 11th Rifle Brigade. Henson was a natural impresario, Gilbey was not only a war hero who had won the M.C. at Loos but a talented performer and a prolific composer of songs and musical sketches, while Eldridge coached the orchestra to a high professional standard. The opening number performed by the entire company, set the scene.

Verey Lights – Verey Lights – V-E-R-E-Y.
Carnoy Camp may be damp,
But the Colosseum's dry.
Now you know where to go
To enjoy yourselves at night.
As you are near us,
Just come and hear us
For we are the VEREY LIGHTS.

You can leave the war outside the door
When you come to our show.
Forget the Huns, their shells and guns

We'll make your troubles go.
Fritz may send up his S.O.S
Lots of green and white.
But the lights they send up best
Are the VEREY LIGHTS.

The words precisely summed up the purpose and the value of concert parties, and the reason the Army encouraged them. There was never a shortage of performers, for the age of mass-entertainment had not yet dawned and there was a wealth of talent among the soldiers, brought up in a society in which people provided their own amusement and anyone who could play an instrument, or who had a pass-able voice was expected to entertain. If they could neither play nor sing they would be called on to recite, and book-shops did a steady trade in collections of comic or dramatic 'recitations', to be learned by heart and declaimed at the next local concert, church 'social', or family gathering. There were many professional entertainers in the Army. Nat Ayer was a star of the musical theatre of the day, so too was Basil Hallam, better known, as a result of his smash-hit comic song, as *'Gilbert the Filbert'*; Leslie Henson was serving in the Army; Ronald Coleman, who later became a Hollywood star, was in the London Scottish and the youthful 'Duggie' Jones, who would also find fame in Hollywood as 'Aubrey Herbert', was in the Rifle Brigade. There were literally thousands of lesser lights who were more than willing to perform – though not all of them found favour with the concert party organisers, who could afford to be fussy. Corporal Jim Pickard, who was with the 76th Winnipeg Grenadiers had a humiliating experience when he tried to join the Dumbbells:

The first time I saw them was after the Battle of Vimy Ridge when we were out on rest – and what a reception they got. The men went wild when they heard these old songs. Some of the artistes were outstanding. Red Newman used to sing '*Oh, it's a lovely War*', and it brought the house down. We had another comedian, Bud Rafferty, and his speciality was '*Lips that touch kippers shall never touch mine*' and '*Where do flies go in the winter time?*' Everyone was singing these songs, you know, and we picked them up on the mouth organ. It was really a wonderful evening to see the Dumbbells. The regulations were supposed to be that the chaps performing had to be unfit for front line service, but Captain Plunkett ran it and he talked to me about joining them. I said, Well, I'd be glad to get out of this front line business. So I did take part in some of these Dumbbell evenings. There was a lad in our section and he was quite a pianist and we'd been entertaining our own units. I and this other fellow used to sing these old tear jerkers, '*Love me and the world is mine*' and '*When the field is white with daisies I'll return*'. Well the Dumbbells thought we were all right, but our pals in the audience offered us no honour. They gave us the bird, and no mistake. So that was that. But we didn't hold a grudge. Whenever we were out on rest and we heard that the Dumbbells were in the locality, we'd walk miles to hear them, and every performance it seemed they got better. Of course, when Marjorie came on there was pandemonium, it was so very life-like. She was a wonderful impersonator, or rather, he was. They used to do shows for some British Units and a lot of those young British officers wanted to make a date with Marjorie. She was so good that they couldn't be convinced she was a female impersonator.

The big snag for concert parties on Active Service was the lack of females at the Front. Fortunately, it was largely a youthful army and the deficiency could often be made up by some slim, fresh-complexioned youth who seldom, if ever, needed to shave and the charms of 'Marjorie' of the Dumbbells were not unique. On the evening of his debut, the subaltern who took the role of 'leading lady' with '*The Pedlars*' had the unusual experience of being ogled amorously by his own Colonel, seated in the front row, and his wicked brother officers even arranged a formal intro-duction at the interval. Fortunately the Colonel had a sense of humour.

'Female' performers were eagerly sought after, and the Balmorals of the 51st Division, with the connivance of their Colonel contrived to kidnap a desirable lovely from the 32nd Division. They were due to leave Senlis and the 32nd Division were staying on. They had no concert party and no plans to start one. A young soldier of the H.L.I named Connel had seen *The Balmorals* show and wanted to join them. He had been a professional impersonator before the war and was a first-class performer, but the 32nd wouldn't hear of transferring, or even loaning him. So, with the collusion of their senior officers, *The Balmorals* kidnapped him. The 32nd Division did not take this kindly, but the 51st had no intention of giving up their prize. The

Divisional Commander solved the problem by inviting the Army Commander and staff to dinner and taking them to the show with 'Isabelle de Hotstuff' in the starring role. What was the good of wasting such talent, he pointed out. So, 'Isabelle', with the Army's consent became officially one of the 51st Division's gunners and continued to wow her audience for the rest of the war!

Nowhere were shows more eagerly anticipated and appreciated than in prisoner of war camps – and nowhere were men more starved of female company. With none of the hazards of Active Service to distract them, and ample time to rehearse and polish their shows, the officers incarcerated in Freiburg P.O.W. camp in southern Germany ran what amounted to a repertory company. The F.A.D.S – Freiburg Amateur Dramatic Society – put on regular shows ranging from Shakespearean melodrama to light comedy and variety shows. They too had their 'lovelies' to fill the female roles and the flirtatious performance of one subaltern was habitually greeted with such an uproar of cheers and whistles, that he literally stopped the show. He also inspired a ditty, performed in the style of a Victorian ballad, that went down almost as well.

> 'Tis true she hath a face that's fair,
> And lip and cheek rose-red,
> And golden tresses, rich and rare,
> In silken waves be-spread;
> True that with sweet seraphic smile
> A soft love song she'll sing;
> And to the gallant's heart awhile
> A sense of yearning bring

> But oft I've caught a glimpse of her
> In careless disarray –
> And things are not what they appear
> Behind the footlights gay.
> Though sparkling eyes and rouged cheek
> Bespeak a goddess fair,
> 'Tis fools alone such shadows seek,
> they'll find no substance there.
> Therefore beware this bold FAD lass,
> Though it seems more than kind,
> Strive not the closed stage door to pass –
> I know! I've been behind!!

In far-off Salonika, where the troops fighting the 'sideshow' on the Balkan front felt almost as cut off as the prisoners of war, they did manage to find the genuine article for one show that toured the back-areas, and in which a comedian dressed as a Greek labour-gang foreman sang a hilarious song entitled 'Hi there, Johnny'. Then someone had the felicitous idea of recruiting a genuine labour-corps Greek for the part. Captain Seligman was in the audience.

> An elderly man of dignified appearance with white whiskers, he trod the boards with the stateliness which can only be acquired by a ten-year study of the part of Hamlet. Suddenly he discarded his dignity and, with a wink at the delighted audience, advanced gallantly towards the leading 'lady' and kissed her hand. Encircling her slim waist with Victorian courtesy, he accompanied her in a Macedonian gavotte. Then, with the same old-world grace, he

took leave of his partner and danced by himself. <u>Never</u> have I seen an audience so convulsed with laughter! He played the part for six nights before he retired from the stage and went back to breaking stones on the Seres road.

The musical theatre was thriving on the home front, not only musical plays like *Chu Chin Chow* which ran for almost the whole of the war years, but traditional music hall and the ever-popular revues like *The Bing Boys* starring the pin-up Violet Loraine singing '*If You Were the Only Girl in the World*', and the even more glamorous Teddy Gerard whose photograph, like that of Gladys Cooper, was pinned to a muddy wall in a thousand dug-outs. Teddy's theme song made much of the fact that her surname, given a slight alteration in spelling, was also the designation of a London telephone exchange and, before the introduction of automatic dialling, both name and number had to be given to connect the call.

> *Everybody calls me Teddy,*
> *T-E double D-Y,*
> *Naughty, sporty, never, never haughty,*
> *With an R.S.V.P. eye.*
> *All day long the telephone,*
> *Keeps on ringing hard;*
> *Are you there, little Teddy bear,*
> *Naughty, naughty one Gerard?*

Soldiers on leave in their home towns went, as a matter of course, to the theatre or the music hall and when they returned to the front the songs they had heard went with them, either by means of gramophone recordings, sheet music, or simply happy recollection. Many a signaller, who was unfortunate enough to be working on a telegraph pole when a bunch of soldiers passed by, was regaled with a raucous chorus of either *'Naughty, naughty one Gerard'* or another, equally popular song celebrating Kitty the telephone operator, *'Kitty, Kitty isn't it a pity that you have to work so hard...'*

But there was also nostalgia and moments of longing that were hard to bear. Dorothy Nicol, who was nursing at a Base hospital on the coast, remembered one particular evening.

> The wounded had their own hospital concerts, so this one was for 'Troops Only' and the Tommies came from all the base units for miles around. Apart from two rows in front reserved for nurses, there wasn't a square inch of the rest of the hall that wasn't khaki. They sat on shelves, they stood on window-ledges. When there were no chairs left, they sat on the floor. The atmosphere was unbelievably excited as the audience waited, and then absolute silence when the concert itself began. They roared with laughter at every allusion, they joined in every chorus and brought the house down with thunderous applause. One little man came on and sang *'Old King Cole'* in the manner of an ordinary soldier, then various ranks (*'The Colonel has a very fine swear, and a very fine swear has he, and he blankety blanks, and blankety blanks and calls for his subalterns three'*, and the Adjutant calls for his horse, and the captains demand three months leave, and the

subalterns complain that they do all the work). In between the turns there were always choruses of popular songs and everyone joined in. It was terribly moving to hear these hundreds of men singing in unison, and sometimes it cut you to the heart. There was such tension, such emotion, such nostalgia. The pianist started to play *'The Long, Long Trail.'*

> *There's a long, long trail a-winding*
> *Into the land of my dreams,*
> *Where the nightingales are singing,*
> *And a white moon beams...*

I looked out of the window and saw a stream of ambulances going very slowly along the dusty road. At the same time, through the other window overlooking the railway line, I could see a train full of men with horses and guns going up the line. It wasn't the first train of the evening – it was just before Passchendaele, and they'd been rumbling past all through the concert – but that one going by, just when they were singing that song, overwhelmed me. It was too much, seeing the ambulances coming in and the train going up at the same time – too much to think of all the pain and hurt and suffering.

So many years on, to a generation which looks back with compassion on the horrors of the Great War, that description strikes a sympathetic chord. It is harder to appreciate the lighter side, which was so important to the soldiers themselves. They were not callous. Of course they were not – and the few survivors do not see themselves as victims any more than their comrades did. Their attitude is best summed up in the lines; '*And still we laughed in Amiens, as dead men laughed a week ago/ What cared we if in Delville Wood the splintered trees saw Hell below?/ We cared. We cared! But laughter runs/ The sweetest stream a man may know/ To rinse him from the taint of guns.*' (From *Song of Amiens* by T. P. Cameron Wilson.)

The music, the laughter and, above all, the songs of the First World War, have been described as 'a protest of life against death', but perhaps they merely represent the ascendancy of the human spirit over the cruel inhumanity of the war itself. The songs are still remembered, and some still sung almost a century after the start of that 'Great War' that still haunts succeeding generations. That surely is a kind of immortality and, in a sense, a fitting memorial to those men who marched to war in a forgotten world.

1914: PATRIOTIC SONGS

GOODBYE DOLLY GRAY

This rousing song was written in 1898 by Will D. Cobb with music by Paul Barnes. First sung by the troops who went off to the Boer War, it was again sung by the British Expeditionary Force as it left for France in 1914, doubtless because the regimental bands which played them off thought it was appropriate.

I have come to say goodbye, Dolly Gray
It's no use to ask me why, Dolly Gray.
There's a murmur in the air
You can hear it ev'rywhere,
It is time to do or dare, Dolly Gray.
Don't you hear the tramp of feet, Dolly Gray
Sounding thro' the village street, Dolly Gray
'Tis the tramp of soldiers' feet in their uniforms so neat
'So goodbye until we meet, Dolly Gray!'

CHORUS
Goodbye Dolly, I must leave you,
Tho' it breaks my heart to go
Something tells me I am needed at the front to fight the foe.
See the soldier boys are marching,
And I can no longer stay
Hark! I hear the bugle calling,
'Goodbye Dolly Gray! Gray! Gray!'

Hear the rolling of the drums, Dolly Gray
Back from the war reg'ment comes, Dolly Gray
On your lovely face so fair
I can see a look of care
For your soldier boy's not there, Dolly Gray
For the one you loved so well, Dolly Gray
In the midst of battle fell, Dolly Gray

With his face towards the foe as he died he murmured low,
'I must say goodbye and go, Dolly Gray!'

CHORUS
Goodbye Dolly, I must leave you, (etc.)

COME ON AND JOIN

Tune: *'Alexander's Rag-Time Band'*

At the outbreak of war Lord Kitchener became Secretary of State for War. His stern, moustachioed face was everywhere on the poster with his finger pointing at all young men exhorting them to join up with the emotive phrase 'Your King and Country Need You'.

> Come on and join, come on and join,
> Come on and join Lord Kitchener's army.
> Ten bob a week, plenty grub to eat,
> Bloody great boots make blisters on yer feet.
> Come on and join, come on and join,
> Come on and join Lord Kitchener's army.

The following verse is the Australian alternative. William Hughes became their Prime Minister in 1915.

> Why don't you join, why don't you join,
> Why don't you join Billy Hughes' Army?
> Six bob a day and nothing to eat,
> Great big boots and blisters on your feet,
> Why don't you join, why don't you join,
> Why don't you join Billy Hughes' Army?

SAVE YOUR KISSES TILL THE BOYS COME HOME

Written by Fred Barnes

This is a song exhorting the girls at home to stay faithful until their soldier boys come home!

All the girls are lonely, lonely everywhere
Safe in cosy corners – nothing doing there.
Never mind, never mind, don't you worry or sigh
Though your best boy's gone on the RATSA plan
He'll come back a military man
And he'll be the first to catch your eye.
Never mind little girlie, never mind.

CHORUS
Save your kisses till the Boys come home,
When the Boys come home
They'll be everybody's darlings.
You must say goodbye to the fellows dressed in flannel
Keep your love for the boys who are over the Channel fighting,
They've all missed you for a long long while
And they're lonely over the foam
So girls save all your little kisses till the boys come home.

You can wait a while, girls, till the boys come back,
If he's soldier Tommy, if he's a sailor Jack,
Never mind, never mind, oh there's coming a day,
When the band will play and the flags will fly
Stay at homes will look and wonder why
You are proud of the boy who went away.
Wear a smile, little girlie, just a while.

CHORUS
Save your kisses till the Boys come home, (etc.)

RATSA was a Royal Artillery training course for new recruits at the beginning of the War.

WE DON'T WANT TO LOSE YOU

Words and music by Paul A. Rubens

Written in 1914, this patriotic song, sung in the music halls by Phyllis Dare, undoubtedly stirred the conscience of many young men and helped swell the ranks of Kitchener's army. At concerts given for the benefit of new recruits, they heard innumerable ladies promising 'We'll kiss you/ When you come back again.' There was, though, a minor sensation when one of the earliest of the wounded from Mons walked up to the stage and demanded from a pretty singer the fulfilment of her promise!

We've watched you playing cricket
And every kind of game
At football golf and polo,
You men have made your name,
But now your country calls you
To play your part in war,
And no matter what befalls you
We shall love you all the more,
So, come and join the forces
As your fathers did before.

CHORUS
Oh! we don't want to lose you
But we think you ought to go
For your King and Country
Both need you so;
We shall want you and miss you
But with all our might and main
We shall cheer you, thank you, kiss you
When you come back again.

We want you from all quarters
So, help us South and North
We want you in your thousands,
From Falmouth to the Forth,
You'll never find us fail you
When you are in distress,
So, answer when we hail you,
And let your word be 'Yes'
And so your name, in years to come
Each mother's son shall bless.

CHORUS
Oh! we don't want to lose you (etc.)

It's easy for us women
To stay at home and shout,
But remember, there is a duty
To the men who first went out.
The odds against that handful
Were nearly four to one,
And we cannot rest until
It's man for man, and gun for gun!
And every woman's duty
Is to see their duty done.

CHORUS
Oh! we don't want to lose you (etc.)

However many soldiers soon became fed up with the song and adapted it to their own words as is shown in these two verses.

For we don't want your loving,
And we think you're awfully slow
To see that we don't want you,
So please won't you go.
We don't like your sing songs,
And we loathe your refrain,
So don't you dare to sing it
Near us again.

Now we don't want to hurry you,
But it's time you ought to go;
For your songs and your speeches
They bore us so.
Your coaxings and pettings
Drive us nigh insane;
Oh! we'll hate you, boo you and hiss you
If you sing it again.

I'LL MAKE A MAN OF YOU

The original song, written by Arthur Wimperis with music by Herman Finck, was in the 1914 revue, 'The Passing Show', and sung by Gwendoline Brogden at the London Hippodrome. Written five months before the outbreak of the First World War it was not intended as a recruiting song, but of course with the outbreak of war it became a gift to the recruiting campaign. It was popular because of its slightly risqué chorus; Maggie Smith gave a memorably suggestive rendering of the song in the 1969 film, 'Oh! What a Lovely War'.

The army and the navy need attention,
The outlook isn't healthy you'll admit,
But I've got a perfect dream of a new recruiting scheme,
Which I really think is absolutely it.
If only other girls would do as I do
I believe that we could manage it alone,
For I turn all suitors from me but the sailor and the Tommy,
I've an army and a navy of my own.

CHORUS
On Sunday I walk out with a soldier,
On Monday I'm taken by a Tar,
On Tuesday I'm out with a baby Boy Scout,
On Wednesday a Hussar,
On Thursday I gang oot wi' a Scottie,
On Friday, the Captain of the crew,
But on Saturday I'm willing
If you'll only take the shilling,
To make a man of every one of you.

I teach the tenderfoot to face the powder
That adds an added lustre to my skin,
And I show the raw recruit how to give a chaste salute,
So when I'm presenting arms he's falling in,
It makes you almost proud to be a woman
When you make a strapping soldier of a kid,
And he says 'You put me through it and I didn't want to do it,
But you went and made me love you, so I did.'

CHORUS
On Sunday I walk out with a Bo'sun,
On Monday a Rifleman in green,
On Tuesday I choose a 'sub' in the 'Blues',
On Wednesday a Marine;
On Thursday, a Terrier from Tooting,
On Friday, a Midshipman or two,
But on Saturday I'm willing
If you'll only take the shilling,
To make a man of every one of you.

The soldiers' rude version is shown below.

On Monday I touched her on the ankle,
On Tuesday I touched her on the knee,
On Wednesday I confess, I lifted up her dress.
On Thursday I saw it, gorblimey,
On Friday I put me 'and upon it,
On Saturday she gave my balls a treat,
On Sunday after supper, I whopped me fucker up 'er
An' now I'm paying forty bob a week! Gorblimey.

New recruits were given a shilling for expenses when they signed up.

GOODBYE JENNY

A powerful Scottish song made famous by the music hall star Hetty King.

Sandy felt as swanky as the Duke of Killiekrankie,
For young Sandy had enlisted for the War,
But Jenny by his side,
Her sorrow could not hide,
While gazing at her laddie big and braw.
Just take this sprig of heather, it's the luckiest of charms,
She whispered, then he answered
As he took her in his arms –

CHORUS
Goodbye Jenny, I must gang awa',
Because my King is needin' laddies
Big and braw,
Hear them shouting, as they go,
Are we downhearted – No!
Goodbye Jenny, when I'm far awa',
You need not frown,
For I'll wear your sprig of heather
In my old Scotch hat,
When we march through Berlin town!

Jenny looked at Sandy,
For he really looked so dandy,
And young Sandy grew as fine as fine could be,
Said he, 'You may be sure
The War will soon be o'er

Once the Germans catch a glimpse o' me.'
But though he joked and laughed aloud
His heart was full of pain.
Tenderly he kissed her as he whispered once again…

CHORUS
Goodbye Jenny, I must gang awa', (etc.)

J.H. DOWD.

WHEN BELGIUM PUT THE KIBOSH ON THE KAISER

Written and composed in 1914 by Alf Ellerton

The Kaiser invaded Belgium on 1 August 1914, thereby bringing Britain into the war: Belgium fought bravely but could not halt the German juggernaut without Allied help.

A silly German sausage dreamt Napoleon he'd be
Then went and broke his promise,
It was made in Germany,
He shook hands with Britannia
And eternal peace he swore;
Naughty boy! He talked of peace
While he prepared for war.
He stirred up little Serbia
To serve his dirty trick,
But dirty nights at Liege quite
Upset this Dirty Dick.
His luggage labell'd England
And his programme nicely set,
He shouted 'First stop Paris!'
But he hasn't got there yet,
For—

CHORUS
Belgium put the 'Kibosh' on the Kaiser;
Europe took a stick and made him sore;
On his throne it hurts to sit,
And when John Bull starts to hit,
He will never sit up on it any more!
Belgium put the 'Kibosh' on the Kaiser;
Europe took a stick and made him sore;
He'll be banished to the woods,

And we'll bar his German goods,
And we'll never drink his lager anymore!
His warships sail'd upon the sea,
They looked a pretty sight,
But when they heard a bulldog bark
They disappeared from sight.
The Kaiser said, 'Be careful!
If by Jellicoe they're seen
Ev'ry man-of-war I've got
Will be a submarine.'
We chased his ships to Turkey
And the Kaiser startled stood,
Scratched his head and said,
'Don't hurt! You see I'm touching wood.'
Then Turkey bought the warships
Just to aid the German plot.
Be careful, Mister Turkey,
Or you'll do the Turkey trot.
For—

CHORUS
Belgium put the 'Kibosh' on the Kaiser;
Europe took a stick and made him sore;
When we enter Germany,
'Knock the Kaiser' it will be;
Oh, it won't be 'Hoch der Kaiser' anymore!
Belgium put the 'Kibosh' on the Kaiser;
Europe took a stand and made him sore;
And if Turkey makes a stand
She'll get Ghurka'd and Japann'd
And her views she'll never air 'em any more!

He'll have to go to school again
And learn his geography,
Quite forgot Australia
And the 'hands across the sea.'
India and Canada,

The Russian and the Jap,
And England look'd so small
He couldn't see it on the map.
Whilst Ireland seem'd unsettled,
'Ah!' said he, 'I'll settle John,'
But he didn't know the Irish
Like he knew them later on
Tho' the Kaiser stirr'd the lion,
Please excuse him from the crime;
His lunatic attendant
wasn't with him at the time.
When—

CHORUS
Belgium put the 'Kibosh' on the Kaiser; (etc)

HERE WE ARE! HERE WE ARE AGAIN!

Written in 1914 by Charles Knight and composed by Kenneth Lyle, this became a hugely successful song among the soldiers, and from innumerable sing-songs, the Tommies would know all the words.

The poets, since the War began,
Have written lots of things
About our gallant soldier lads
Which no one ever sings.
Although their words are very good,
The lilt they seem to miss;
For Tommy likes a tricky song,
The song that goes like this —

CHORUS
Here we are! Here we are! Here we are again!
There's Pat and Mac and Tommy and Jack and Joe.

When there's trouble brewing,
When there's something doing
Are we downhearted?
NO! Let 'em all come!
Here we are! Here we are! Here we are again!
We're fit and well, and feeling right as rain.
Never mind the weather,
Now then, all together,
Hullo! Hullo! Here we are again!

When Tommy went across the sea,
To bear the battle's brunt,
Of course he sang this little song
While marching to the front.
And when he's walking through Berlin,
He'll sing the anthem still;
He'll shove a 'Woodbine' on, and say,
'How are you, Uncle Bill?'

CHORUS
Here we are! Here we are! Here we are again! (etc.)

And when the boys have finished up
With Hermann and with Max,
And when the enemy' got it
Where the chicken got the axe,
The girls will all be waiting
'Midst the cheering and the din,
To hear their sweethearts singing,
As the ship comes sailing in —

CHORUS
Here we are! Here we are! Here we are again! (etc.)

'Uncle Bill' is Kaiser Wilhelm II – a grandson of Queen Victoria.

KEEP THE HOME FIRES BURNING

Of the three songs that most vividly evoke the First World War (the other two being 'Tipperary' and 'Roses of Picardy') perhaps the most interesting is 'Keep the Home Fires Burning'.

The tune and the key phrase of the chorus – 'Keep the Home Fires Burning' – were written by a twenty-one-year-old Royal Naval Air Service pilot, Ivor Novello. The lyrics were by an American poet, Lena Guilbert Ford, who was living in London at the time. The song was written in 1914, when enthusiasm for the war was at its height. Its emotional impact on families was enormous throughout the war; there was hardly a household that had not seen a father or son go off to the war.

The immense popularity of the song brought Ivor Novello back to the Home Front to help the war effort by writing more morale-raising songs. and to compose for West End revues that entertained Londoners and troops on home leave. He went on to write a succession of hit musicals from the mid 1930s to the early fifties.

> They were summoned from the hillside,
> They were called in from the glen,
> And the country found them ready
> At the stirring call for men.
> Let no tears add to their hardship,
> As the soldiers pass along,
> And although your heart is breaking
> Make it sing this cheery song.

> *CHORUS*
> *Keep the Home fires burning,*
> *While your hearts are yearning,*
> *Though your lads are far away they dream of home.*
> *There's a silver lining*
> *Through the dark cloud shining,*
> *Turn the dark cloud inside out,*
> *Till the boys come home.*

Overseas there came a pleading,
'Help a Nation in distress!'
And we gave our glorious laddies;
Honour bade us do no less.
For no gallant son of Britain
To a foreign yoke shall bend,
And no Englishman is silent
To the sacred call of Friend.

CHORUS
Keep the Home fires burning, (etc.)

HOME FRONT AND
MUSIC HALL SONGS

WHO WERE YOU WITH LAST NIGHT?

This song was written in 1912 by Fred Godfrey and Mark Sheridan and was extremely popular,   particularly the chorus, with soldiers at the beginning of the war.

In an office up the West,
Obadiah, smartly dressed,
Wandered in one Friday morn,
In a brand new fancy vest.
His pals all rose and said
My word, you're a naughty, naughty boy.
Last night we saw you making eyes at a nice little lump of joy,
You kissed her twice on the same place twice,
And gave her waist a squeeze,
So we'd like to inform us mister
Obadiah, please!

CHORUS
Who were you with last night?
Who were you with last night?

It wasn't your sister, it wasn't your ma,
Ah! Ah! Ah! Ah! Ah! Ah! Ah! Ah!
Who were you with last night?
Out in the pale moonlight
Are you going to tell your missus when you get home,
Who were you with last night?

Like a rosy apple red,
Obadiah blushed and said,
You're mistaken, boys, because
I was out with Uncle Fred.
His pals looked round and winked,
Then said, as they gave a knowing grin,
Do you always squeeze your Uncle's waist, and tickle his bristly chin,
Does your Uncle, too, wear a high heeled shoe,
And a dainty powdered face,
Does he sport a hobble skirt and bits of
Furbelows and lace?

CHORUS
Who were you with last night?(etc.)

Obadiah said, 'I'm sure,
My brother, pr'aps, you fellows saw,'
They said Wow-wow Obadiah,
You can tell that tale to Noah,
We knew you by your sprightly walk,
And the tale you told was grand.
Last night we saw you in the park there listening to the band.
Your darling wife, she would save your life,
And put your hair in curl,
If she knew you'd been out walking with some
Other little girl!

CHORUS
Who were you with last night?(etc.)

HITCHY KOO

Written in 1912 by L. Wolfe Gilbert with music by Muir and Abrahams

In the early months of the war there was something of a pause in the supply of popular tunes. The Tommies simply sang the favourites of the day, such as 'Hitchy Koo' and 'Who Were You With Last Night?'

If you've got an ear for music then just gather near,
Tell me, can't you hear it buzzin' in your ear?
Is it music? Sure it's music, it's the best you'll ever hear,
It's ever-lovin' honey calling baby dear,
Say, ain't that music weird, strangest you ever heard?
Say, don't you be skeered, listen!

CHORUS
Oh! Ev'ry ev'ning hear him sing,
It's the cutest little thing,
Got the cutest little swing,
Hitchy koo, hitchy koo, hitchy koo.
Oh! Simply meant for kings and queens,
Don't you ask me what it means,
I just love that hitchy koo, hitchy koo, hitchy koo.
Say, he does it just like no one could,
When he does it, say, he does it good.
Oh! Ev'ry ev'ning hear him sing,
It's the cutest little thing,
Got the cutest little swing,
Hitchy koo, hitchy koo, hitchy koo.

Oh! It acts just like a tonic to my love sick heart,
I cannot wait till ev'ning till that thing will start;
Do I love it? Sure I love it, of my life it is a part,
Like the voice of Cupid sending me his little dart,

Say, ain't that music weird, strangest you ever heard?
Say, don't you be skeered, listen!

CHORUS
Oh! Ev'ry ev'ning hear him sing, (etc.)

KEEP YOUR HEAD DOWN, ALLEYMAN

Tune: '*Hold Your Hand out Naughty Boy*'
Composed by C.W. Murphy and Worton David

'*Hold your Hand out Naughty Boy*' was the music hall hit of the British
Expeditionary Force in 1914.

The original song:

> *Hold your hand out naughty boy,*
> *Hold your hand out naughty boy!*
> *Last night in the pale moonlight,*
> *I saw you! I saw you!*
> *You were spooning in the park*
> *With a nice girl in the dark,*
> *And you said you'd never kissed a girl before*
> *Hold your hand out naughty boy.*

The parody: ('Alleyman' is a corruption of the French 'Allemand', a
German).

> Keep your head down, Alleyman,
> Keep your head down, Alleyman,
> Last night, in the pale moonlight
> We saw you, we saw you,
> You were mending broken wire
> When we opened rapid fire,
> If you want to see your father in that Fatherland
> Keep your head down, Alleyman.

HELLO! HELLO! WHO'S YOUR LADY FRIEND?

Written in 1913 by David Worton and Bert Lee and composed by
Harry Fragson

This song became an immense success in the summer of 1914, and the
soldiers sung it lustily, particularly the chorus, as they marched to war.

Jeremiah Jones, a lady's man was he,
Every pretty girl he loved to spoon;
Till he found a wife and down beside the sea
Went to Margate for the honeymoon;
But when he strolled along the promenade
With his little wife just newly wed,
He got an awful scare when someone strolling there,
Came up to him and winked and said —

CHORUS
Hello! Hello! Who's your lady friend?
Who's the little girlie by your side?
I've seen you with a girl or two
Oh! Oh! Oh! I am surprised at you;
Hello! Hello! Stop your little games
Don't you think your ways you ought to mend?
It isn't the girl I saw you with at Brighton
Who, who, who's your lady friend?

Jeremiah took his wife's mamma one night,
Round to see a moving picture show;
There upon the screen a picture came in sight,
Jeremiah cried 'He'd better go!'
For on that picture was Jeremiah

With a pretty girl upon his knee;
Ma cried, 'What does it mean?' Then pointing to the screen,
The people yelled at Jones with glee —

CHORUS
Hello! Hello! Who's your lady friend?(etc.)

Jeremiah now has settled down in life,
Said goodbye to frills and furbelows;
Never thinks of girls except his darling wife,
Always takes her everywhere he goes
By jove, why! There he is you naughty boy!
With a lady too, you're rather free
Of course, you'll stake your life, the lady is your wife
But tell me on the strict Q.T. —

CHORUS
Hello! Hello! Who's your lady friend?(etc.)

Christmas pantomime were Jones's chief delight,
Once he madly loved the Fairy Queen;
There behind the scenes, he spoon'd with her one night,
Someone for a lark pulled up the scenes,
And there was poor old Jones up on the stage
With his arm around the lady fair;
The house began to roar from gallery down to floor
Then everybody shouted there —

CHORUS
Hello! Hello! Who's your lady friend?(etc.)

CHARLOTTE THE HARLOT

Tune: *'Gilbert the Filbert'*

'Gilbert the Filbert' was Captain Basil Hallam Radford, a West End actor, whose song was hugely popular in 1914. He joined up and, as an observer in a kite-balloon unit, was killed on 30th August 1916 at Ville-sur-Ancre, when his balloon cable snapped and his parachute failed to open when he jumped.

The original song:
> *I am Gilbert, the Filbert,*
> *The knut with a k,*
> *The pride of Piccadilly*
> *And blasé roué!*
> *Oh Hades,*
> *The ladies*
> *All leave their wooden huts*
> *For Gilbert, the Filbert*
> *The Colonel of the (K)nuts.*

The soldiers' version turned into a marching song:
> I'm Charlotte the Harlot
> The Queen of the whores,
> The pride of Piccadilly
> All covered in sores;
> Oh! You should smell me
> When I lift up my drawers,
> I'm Charlotte the Harlot
> The Queen of the whores.

IT'S A LONG WAY TO TIPPERARY

Composed by Jack Judge in 1912, with music by Harry Williams

The hit song of the First World War. Judge, a market stall holder, wrote the song for a bet and later made a considerable income out of it, including a pension from the publishers which he received until his death in 1938. Judge had never been to Ireland before but his grandparents lived there. The song was originally introduced into the Army by the Connaught Rangers who had been stationed in Tipperary before the war. The song was heard by the *Daily Mail* correspondent, George Curnock, at Boulogne in August 1914 'as a company of Connaught Rangers passed us singing with a note of strange pathos in their rich Irish voices, a song that I never heard before'. His report ensured the song's immortality.

Up to mighty London came an Irishman one day,
As the streets are paved with gold, sure everyone was gay;
Singing songs of Piccadilly, Strand and Leicester Square,
Till Paddy got excited, then he shouted to them there –

CHORUS
It's a long way to Tipperary,
It's a long way to go;
It's a long way to Tipperary,
To the sweetest girl I know!
Goodbye Piccadilly,
Farewell Leicester Square,
It's a long long way to Tipperary
But my heart's right there!

Paddy wrote a letter to his Irish Molly O
Saying, 'Should you not receive it, write and let me know!'
'If I make mistakes in spelling, Molly dear', said he,

'Remember it's the pen that's bad, don't lay the blame on me.'

CHORUS
It's a long way to Tipperary, (etc.)
Molly wrote a neat reply to Irish Paddy O,
Saying, 'Mike Maloney wants to marry me, and so
Leave the Strand and Piccadilly, or you'll be to blame,
For love has fairly drove me silly – hoping you're the same!'

CHORUS
It's a long way to Tipperary, (etc.)

Although hugely popular at the beginning of the war, and it remained so throughout the war on the Home Front, the song was soon parodied by the soldiers:

That's the wrong way to tickle Marie,
That's the wrong way to kiss!
Don't you know that over here, lad,
They like it best like this!
Hooray pour le Français!
Farewell, Angleterre!
We didn't know the way to tickle Marie,
But we learned how, over there!

PACK UP YOUR TROUBLES IN YOUR OLD KIT BAG

One of the most famous of all First World War songs. This rousing marching song was written in 1915 by George Asat and Felix Powell. Old-fashioned in phrasing and philosophy, it is the story of Private Perks, a born survivor. He is the artful dodger who can always scrounge rations, and he has a winning smile even in adversity. The song also pays tribute to the soldier's pick-me-up – a comforting cigarette.

'Lucifer' (matches) were in short supply. Before the advent of safety matches, they could only be sent to France with and under the same stringent conditions as munitions – therefore they were much-prized and needed for lighting cigarettes, cookers, fires and candles in dug-outs and billets. Hence the invention of the 'trench lighter', with its wick and flint.

> Private Perks is a funny little codger
> With a smile, a funny smile.
> Five feet none, he's an artful little dodger
> With a smile, a sunny smile.
> Flush or broke,
> He'll have his little joke,
> He can't be surpress'd
> All the other fellows have to grin
> When he gets this off his chest, Hi!

> *CHORUS*
> *Pack up your troubles in your old kit bag,*
> *And smile, smile, smile.*
> *While you've a lucifer to light your fag,*
> *Smile, boys, that's your style.*
> *What's the use of worrying?*

It never was worthwhile,
So pack up your troubles in your old kit bag,
And smile, smile, smile.

Private Perks went a-marching into Flanders
With his smile, his funny smile.
He was loved by the privates and commanders
For his smile, his sunny smile.
When a throng of Germans came along,
With a mighty swing,
Perks yell'd out, 'This little bunch is mine!'
Keep your heads down, boys and sing, Hi!

CHORUS
Pack up your troubles in your old kit bag, (etc.)

Private Perks he came back from Boche shooting
With his smile, his funny smile.
Round his home he then set about recruiting
With his smile, his sunny smile.
He told all his pals, the short, the tall,
What a time he'd had;
And as each enlisted like a man,
Private Perks said 'Now, my lad', Hi!

CHORUS
Pack up your troubles in your old
  kit bag, (etc.)

ANOTHER LITTLE DRINK WOULDN'T DO US ANY HARM

This popular music hall ballad, considered quite risqué at the time, was written by Clifford Grey in 1913. 'Mr Asquith' was Prime Minister until late 1916. His eldest son Raymond, a Grenadier Guards officer, was killed in action on 15 September 1916, during the second phase of the Battle of the Somme. Before 1914, because of his propensity for drink, Herbert Asquith was known as 'Squiff'.

There was a pretty lass and I'm grieved to say,
She climbed upon a 'bus on a windy day,
When a busy little breeze blew an awful storm,
And another little drink wouldn't do us any harm.

CHORUS
Another little drink, another little drink,
Another little drink wouldn't do us any harm
Another little drink, another little drink
Another little drink, wouldn't do us any harm

With our local curate once to our sewing bee I went
When the lights all went out, there was no harm meant,
He did some fancy work and we sang a little psalm,
And another little drink wouldn't do us any harm.

CHORUS
Another little drink, another little drink, (etc.)

Now in Parliament when they get into a stew,
And they're all mixed and they don't know what to do,
Mr. Asquith says in a manner sweet and calm,
'Well, another little drink wouldn't do us any harm.'

CHORUS
Another little drink, another little drink, (etc.)

I went to a ball dressed as the map of France,
Said a girl 'show me how the French advance',
When she reached the firing line I shouted in alarm,
And another little drink wouldn't do us any harm.

CHORUS
Another little drink, another little drink, (etc.)

MY OLD IRON CROSS

Tune: *'The Man who Broke the Bank at Monte Carlo'*

This was performed by Harry Champion, a well known music hall star. By 1915, music hall performers realised that they couldn't continue to ignore the War, and mocked anything German from the Kaiser to the language.

I'm the bloke that broke the bank at Monte Carlo,
I'm the hero of a dozen dirty nights,
I went out in a submarine to give the Kaiser one,
It went off bang and up I went and landed in the Sun.
There I met the Kaiser and he said 'I'm up the stick'
'If you get me out of here I'll treat you mighty quick'.

CHORUS
Oh my old Iron Cross, my old Iron Cross,
What a waste I do declare,
Over there in Germany they're giving them away,

You can have a dozen if you shout 'Hooray'
The Kaiser said to me 'Old Cock,'
'My Kingdom for a horse'
I gave him the one missus dried the clothes on
And he gave me the old Iron Cross.

I've been busy as a bee at building trenches
But I stopped because I wore away my spade,
I'd been digging for a fortnight with the mud up to my neck,
My clothes all torn and tattered and I looked a perfect wreck.
All at once a thousand Germans shouted 'Give us meat'
I gave them a sausage that I'd dug up for a treat.

CHORUS
Oh my old Iron Cross, my old Iron Cross,
What a waste I do declare,
Over there in Germany they're giving them away,
You can have a dozen if you shout 'Hooray'
The Kaiser shouted 'Meat, meat, meat'
I gave him some of course,
Though he only had a nibble at my old ham bone
He gave me the old Iron Cross.

I was scouting 'round a place called Schemozzel,
With a thousand Russian lancers out for blood,
The officer commanding us had gone to get a drink,
So I sent the cabin boy for one in less than half-a-wink.
Then we stormed the trenches and we made the Germans run,
Captured several prisoners and missed the Kaiser's son.

CHORUS
Oh my old Iron Cross, my old Iron Cross, (etc.)

'Schemozzel' was the soldiers approximation of the pronunciation of the Austro-Hungarian fortress city Przemysl, captured by the Russians and then recaptured.

SEND HIM A CHEERFUL LETTER

Sung by the music hall artist Maie Ash

A sentimental song, but in many ways an essential message to people at home not to cause additional stress by writing about bad news. Letters from home were vitally important to a soldier. There was a terrible sense of helplessness and despair if bad news was received, for there was little they could do, as compassionate leave was not always granted.

I'm thinking, Mrs Atkins, now that Tommy's gone away
You will send him a letter from home.
Don't tell him all your troubles though for instance yesterday,
The children's boots you bought took half your separation pay.
The eldest boy wants trousers and the rent is overdue,
You're planning and you're scheming for of debts you've got a
   few.
But don't you write and tell him, for here's my advice to you
When you send him a letter from home.

CHORUS
Send him a cheerful letter.
Say that it's all OK.
Tell him you've ne'er felt better,
Though it's all the other way.
Don't send a word of sorrow.
Send him a page of joy.
And don't let your tear drops fall upon the kisses
When you write to your soldier boy.

Don't tell him now that mutton's gone to one and two a pound,
When you send him a letter from home.
But tell him for the family the best thing you have found

Is roly-poly pudding, for it easily goes round.
Don't tell him how this morn you plucked a few more new grey
  hairs,
But tell him how your poor old mother tumbled down the stairs.
It may not be the truth, but if it makes him laugh – who cares,
When you send him a letter from home.

CHORUS
Send him a cheerful letter. (etc.)

TAKE ME BACK TO DEAR OLD BLIGHTY

Written in 1916 by A.J. Mills, Fred Godfrey and Bennett Scott

An extremely popular song with the troops, as well as on the Home Front. In the last line of the first verse, there is mention of a gramophone. Apart from rapid movement of armies in France and Flanders during the opening and closing phases of the War, the Western Front was almost static. In these circumstances, there were opportunities for gramophones and records to find their way into rear areas, support lines and even into the trenches themselves. One soldier, Arthur Bliss, who later became master of the Queen's music, wrote after losing his brother in 1916: 'I have suddenly found solace in the gramophone.'

> Jack Dunn son of a gun
> Over in France today,
> Keeps fit doing his bit
> Up to his eyes in clay.
> Each night after a fight
> To pass the time along,
> He's got a little gramophone that plays this song:
>
> *CHORUS*
> *Take me back to dear old Blighty,*
> *Put me on the train for London Town.*
> *Take me over there, drop me anywhere —*
> *Liverpool, Leeds or Birmingham, well I don't care!*
> *I should love to see my best girl,*
> *Cuddling up again we soon shall be; whoa!*
> *Tiddley-iddley ight-y, hurry me home to Blighty;*
> *Blighty is the place for me.*
>
> Bill Spry started to fly
> Up in an aeroplane,
> In France taking a chance

Wish'd he was down again.
Poor Bill feeling so ill
Yell'd out to Pilot Brown,
'Steady a bit, yer fool! We're turning upside down!'

CHORUS
Take me back to dear old Blighty, (etc.)

Jock Lee having his tea
Says to his pal MacFayne,
Look chum, apple and plum!
It's apple and plum again!
Same stuff, isn't it rough?
Fed up with it I am;
Oh! For a pot of Aunt Eliza's raspberry jam!

CHORUS
Take me back to dear old Blighty, (etc.)

One day Micky O'Shea
Stood in a trench somewhere,
So brave having a shave
And trying to part his hair;
Mick yells, dodging the shells, and lumps of dynamite
Talk of Crystal Palace on Firework Night!

CHORUS
Take me back to dear old Blighty, (etc.)

Blighty: England, in the sense of home. The word is thought to be a corruption of the Hindustani *bilaik*, meaning local district.

IF YOU'RE GOING BACK TO BLIGHTY

Tune: *'If You're Going Back to Dixie'*

One of the most famous Home Front songs.

> If you're going back to Blighty
> If you're going back to town,
> In Trafalgar Square, greet the lions there
> Shout 'Hallo, hallo London'.
> Give the man in blue a fiver
> Kiss the girls, don't be afraid,
> Tell every Western Pet
> That she's not forgotten yet
> By the boys of the Old Brigade.

ROSES OF PICARDY

Written in 1916, with words by Fred E. Weatherly and music by Haydn Wood, this poignant ballad reflects the sorrow of parting without lapsing into mawkish sentimentality.

> She is watching by the poplars,
> Colinette with the sea blue eyes,
> She is watching and longing and waiting
> Where the long white roadway lies.
> And a song stirs in the silence,
> As the wind in the boughs above.
> She listens and starts and trembles.
> 'Tis the first little song of love...

> *CHORUS*
> *Roses are shining in Picardy,*
> *In the hush of the silvery dew.*
> *Roses are flow'ring in Picardy,*
> *But there's never a rose like you!*
> *And the roses will die with the summertime,*
> *And our roads may be far apart,*
> *But there's one rose that dies not in Picardy!*
> *'Tis the rose that I keep in my heart!*

> And the years fly on forever,
> 'Til shadows veil their skies,
> But he loves to hold her little hands
> And look in her sea blue eyes.
> And she sees the road by the poplars,
> Where they met in the bygone years,
> For the first little song of the roses
> Is the last little song she hears.

> *CHORUS*
> *Roses are shining in Picardy, (etc.)*

LLOYD GEORGE'S BEER

Sung by Ernie Mayne

After December 1916 when Lloyd George became Prime Minister, many at home, particularly soldiers on leave, thought that the beer had been watered down.

We shall win the war, we shall win the war,
As I've said before, we shall win the war,
The Kaiser's in a dreadful fury,
Now he knows we're making it in every brewery.
Have you read of it? Seen what's said of it?
In 'The Mirror' or 'The Mai'
It's a substitute and a pubstitute,
And it's known as 'Government Ale'.

CHORUS
Lloyd George's beer, Lloyd George's beer,
At the brewery, there's nothing doing,
All the water-works are brewing,
Lloyd George's beer, it isn't dear
Oh they say it's a terrible war, Oh Lor'
And there never was a war like this before
But the worst thing that ever happened in this war
Was Lloyd George's beer.

Buy a lot of it, all they've got of it,
Dip your bread in it, shove you head in it
From January 'till October
And I bet a penny you will still be sober.
Get the froth off it, make your broth of it
With a pair of mutton chops.
Drown your dogs in it, throw some frogs in it
Then you'll see some wonderful hops (in that lovely stuff).

CHORUS
Lloyd George's beer, Lloyd George's beer,
At the brewery, there's nothing doing,
All the water-works are brewing,
Lloyd George's beer, it isn't dear
Said Haig to Joffre when affairs looked black
'If you can't shift the beggars with your gas attack
Get your squirters out and we'll squirt the beggars back
With Lloyd George's beer'.

'Haig' was Commander-in-Chief of the British Army from December 1915 until the end of the war. 'Joffre' was the French Commander-in-Chief. His name is prounced 'Joff-ree' in this song. 'Beggars' was a euphemism for 'buggers'.

BUT FOR GAWD'S SAKE DON'T SEND ME

Written by Gitz Rice in 1917, originally as *'The Conscientious Objector's Lament'*, and performed as a comic song by Alfred Lester in a music hall review called *'Round the Map'*. His 'turn' invariably brought the house down. It was intended to ridicule conscientious objectors, but the chorus was soon being sung with gusto – and sometimes with heartfelt sincerity – by soldiers on active service.

> Perhaps you wonder what I am,
> I will explain to you,
> My conscience is the only thing
> That helps to pull me through.
> Objection is a thing that I
> Have studied thoroughly,
> I don't object to fighting Huns,
> But should hate them fighting me.

CHORUS
Send out the Army and the Navy,
Send out the rank and file,
Send out the brave old Territorials
They'll face the danger with a smile.
Send out the Boys of the Old Brigade,
Who made Old England free,
Send out me brother, me sister and me mother
But for Gawd's sake don't send me.

Non-combatant battalions
Are fairly in my line,
But the Sergeant always hates me
And he calls me 'Baby mine',
But oh, I got so cross with him
I rose to the attack
And when he called me 'Ethel'
I just called him 'Beatrice' back!

CHORUS
Send out the Army and the Navy, etc.

We have a nasty officer,
He is a horrid brute,
Last Friday he was terse with me
'Cos I did not salute.
But I cut him twice today,
Then he asked the reason please?
I said, 'I thought, dear Captain,
That you still were cross with me.'

CHORUS
Send out the Army and the Navy,
Send out the rank and file,
Send out the brave old Territorials
They'll face the danger with a smile.

Send out the Boys of the Old Brigade,
Who made Old England free,
Send out the bakers, and the bloomin' profit-makers
But for Gawd's sake don't send me.

Call out the Army and the Navy
Call out the rank and file.
Call out the brave Territorials
They face danger with a smile!
Call out the King's Militia
They kept England free!
Call out me brother
Me father or me mother
But for Gawd's sake don't call me.

GOOD-BYE-EE!

'*Good-bye-ee!*' was written in 1917 by R.P. Weston and Bert Lee and became an immediate success. It pokes fun at Lieutenant Bertie (amongst others), the stereotypical young subaltern educated at Public School. It contains a fair measure of fashionable slang: 'toodle-oo', 'cheerio, chin chin' for example; 'napoo' is the English strangulation of the French '*il n'y en a plus*' (there is none left).

Brother Bertie went away
To do his bit the other day
With a smile on his lips and his lieutenant 'pips'
Upon his shoulder, bright and gay.
As the train moved out he said
'Remember me to all the birds!'
Then he wagged his paw, and went away to war,
Shouting out these pathetic words —

CHORUS
Good-bye-ee! Good-bye-ee!
Wipe the tear, baby dear,
From your eye-ee.
Though it's hard to part, I know,
I'll be tickled to death to go.
Don't cry-ee! Don't sigh-ee!
There's a silver lining in the sky-ee.
Bonsoir, old thing!
Cheerio! Chin-chin!
Napoo! Toodle-oo! Good-bye-ee!

At a concert down at Kew,
Some convalescents dressed in blue
Had to hear Lady Lee, who had turned eighty-three,
Sing all the old, old songs she knew.
Then she made a speech and said,
'I look upon you boys with pride,
And for what you've done I'm going to kiss each one!'
Then they all grabbed their sticks and cried —

CHORUS
Good-bye-ee! Good-bye-ee! (etc.)

Little Private Patrick Shaw
He was a prisoner of war
Till a Hun with a gun called him 'pig-dog' for fun,
Then Paddy punched him on the jaw.
Right across the barb-wire fence
The German dropped, then, oh dear!
All the wire gave way, and Paddy yelled 'Hooray!'
As he ran for the Dutch frontier —

CHORUS
Good-bye-ee! Good-bye-ee! (etc.)

The British troops parodied this much sung song with their own words at concert parties.

> I heard a funny song one day,
> Sung in a very sloppy way;
> But as it went so fine,
> I wrote this one of mine.
> If it is not sense it's gay.
> For to shove this song I've sighed,
> Every publisher I've tried,
> And to our O.C. I shouted out with glee,
> Just read this! He did, then he cried–

> *CHORUS*
> *Ay, ayee; ay ayee,*
> *Goodness knows, to compose, you've had a try-ee,*
> *To a D.C.M you'll go,*
> *You'll be sentenced to death I know;*
> *Don't cry-ee; don't sigh-ee,*
> *There's still a chance you won't have to die-ee;*
> *Swing the lead, see the Doc,*
> *Say you've got shell-shock,*
> *C'est la guerre; your 'ticket's' there,*
> *Goodbye-ee.*

> The Sergeant-Major read it too.
> He said, 'Of songs I've seen a few,
> As you've worked so hard, do an extra guard,
> Then perhaps a fatigue or two.'
> This made me feel so sick and sad,
> I next pulled up a small French lad,
> I says, 'Look, garçon, compris this new song?'
> He looked at it, then yelled like mad –

> *CHORUS*
> *Good-bye-ee, good-bye-ee.*

OH! IT'S A LOVELY WAR

Written by J.P. Long and Maurice Scott in 1917

Long and Scott's satirical song was the inspiration for Joan Littlewood's remarkable production of *Oh! What A Lovely War* first staged at the Theatre Royal, Stratford in 1963, and filmed by Richard Attenborough in 1969. It shows the marvellous bravado and humour of the Tommy in the face of appalling conditions.

> Up to your waist in water,
> Up to your eyes in slush —
> Using the kind of language,
> That makes your sergeant blush;
> Who wouldn't join the army?
> That's what we all inquire,
> Don't we pity the poor civilians sitting by the fire.

> *CHORUS*
> *Oh! Oh! Oh! it's a lovely war,*
> *Who wouldn't be a soldier eh?*
> *Oh! It's a shame to take the pay.*
> *As soon as 'reveille' has gone*
> *We feel just as heavy as lead,*
> *But we never get up till the sergeant brings*
> *Our breakfast up to bed.*
> *Oh! Oh! Oh! it's a lovely war,*
> *What do we want with eggs and ham*
> *When we've got plum and apple jam?*
> *Form fours! Right turn!*
> *How shall we spend the money we earn?*
> *Oh! Oh! Oh! it's a lovely war.*

When does a soldier grumble?
When does he make a fuss?
No one is more contented
In all the world than us;
Oh! It's a cushy life, boys
Really we love it so
Once a fellow was sent on leave and simply refused to go.

CHORUS
Oh! Oh! Oh! it's a lovely war, (etc.)

Come to the cookhouse door boys,
Sniff at the lovely stew,
Who is it says the Colonel gets better grub than you?
Any complaints this morning?
Do we complain, not we
What's the matter with lumps of onion floating around in tea?

CHORUS
Oh! Oh! Oh! it's a lovely war, (etc.)

SOLDIERS' SONGS FROM THE TRENCHES

WHERE ARE OUR UNIFORMS?

Tune: The hymn *'There is a Happy Land Far, Far Away'*

This hymn was parodied in a number of verses, two of which are shown. It was adopted by Kitchener's Army who drilled and trained for months in their own civvy cloths and shoes until they were issued with Kitchener's Blue — a navy coloured serge cloth. Factories worked flat out to produce khaki cloth but it was an impossible task to produce enough to clothe hundreds of thousands of men overnight. The new recruits had to practise with rifles and even machine guns made of wood. Some were only issued with rifles the day before they left for France. One infantryman told Lyn Macdonald that before he went to France he had only fired six shots. 'Luckily,' he told her, 'when I got there, I discovered I was a good shot.' But Lieutenant Bernard Montgomery, later Field Marshal Viscount Montgomery of Alamein, wrote: 'At least the thing will be over in three weeks.'

Where are our uniforms?
Far, far away.
When will our rifles come?
P'raps, p'raps some day.
All we need is just a gun
For to chase the bloody Hun.
Think of us when we are gone,
Far, far away.

THERE IS A SAUSAGE GUN

Tune: The hymn *'There is a Happy Land Far, Far Away'*

After several months of active service, the songs the Tommies sang changed. On training marches they had sung *'Where are our uniforms? Far, far away…'* for they had wanted to get to the front. Now they were there, and the song took on a more realistic note. A 'sausage gun' was a short range trench mortar (*minenwerfer*), used on the Somme where the trenches were less than thirty yards apart, making normal gunfire ineffective.

> There is a sausage gun
> Over the way.
> Fired by a bloody Hun
> Three times a day.
> You should see the Tommies run
> When they hear that sausage gun
> Fired by a bloody Hun
> Three times a day.

HERE THEY COME

Tune: 'Braganza'

One of the regimental marches of the Royal West Surrey Regiment, this traditional army song originated before the First World War, but was also sung during the war.

Here they come, here they come,
Silly great buggers every one:
Half-a-crown a week to pay
For putting a girl in the family way.

Here they come, here they come,
Second of Foot but second to none.
Here they come, here they come,
Second of Foot but second to none.
Bullshit, bullshit,
Covered from head to foot in it.
Bullshit, bullshit,
Covered from head to foot in it.

Here they come, the dirty lot,
They chased the girls in Aldershot.
Now they're off to Salisbury Plain
To start their dirty work again.

'Aldershot' is a garrison town in Hampshire.
'Salisbury Plain' is where the army carry out manoeuvres.

I'VE LOST MY RIFLE AND MY BAYONET

Tune: *'Since I Lost You'*

I've lost my rifle and my bayonet,
I've lost my pull-through too,
I've lost my disc and my puttees,
I've lost my four-by-two.
I've lost my housewife and hold-all
I've lost my button-stick too.
I've lost my rations and greatcoat —
Sergeant, what shall I do?

I've lost my rifle and bayonet,
I've lost my pull-through too,
I've lost the socks that you sent me
That lasted the whole winter through,
I've lost the razor that shaved me,
I've lost my four-by-two,
I've lost my hold-all and now I've got damn all
Since I've lost you.

THE LONG, LONG TRAIL

Zo Elliott, an American, composed this for a Yale College reunion in 1912. It was published in England at his expense. He was on holiday in Germany in autumn 1914, but got out to Switzerland where he found a considerable sum of money waiting for him, as his song had captured the mood of the moment and had been published world-wide. The haunting words were written by Stoddard King.

Nights are growing very lonely, days are very long;
I'm a-growing weary only list'ning for your song.
Old remembrances are thronging thro' my memory
Thronging till it seems, the world is full of dreams
Just to call you back to me.

CHORUS
There's a long, long trail a-winding
Into the land of my dreams,
Where the nightingales are singing
And a white moon beams:
There's a long, long night of waiting
Until my dreams all come true;
Till the day when I'll be going down
That long, long trail with you.

All night long I hear you calling,
Calling sweet and low;
Seem to hear your footsteps falling ev'rywhere I go.
Tho' the road between us stretches many a weary mile,
Somehow I forget that you're not with me yet
When I think I see you smile.

CHORUS
There's a long, long trail a-winding (etc.)

MY TUNIC IS OUT AT THE ELBOWS

Tune: *'My Bonnie Lies Over the Ocean'*

The word 'puttee' comes from the Hindustani for bandage. It is the cloth wound round the leg from the upper of the boot to near the knee to give support when walking. 'Q.M.' is the abbreviation for Quartermaster.

> My tunic is out at the elbows,
> My trousers are out at the knee,
> My puttees are ragged and frazzled
> But the Q.M. says nothing for me.
>
> My tummy knocks hard on my backbone,
> My dial is thin as can be;
> Still all we get handed at mealtimes,
> Is bully and Maconochie.

SONG OF THE RELUCTANT TRANSPORT DRIVER

Tune: *'My Bonnie Lies Over the Ocean'*

> I've been in the saddle for hours
> I've stuck it as long as I could,
> I've stuck it and stuck it until I said, 'Fuck it,
> My arsehole is not made of wood.'
>
> *CHORUS*
> *Sergeant, Sergeant, oh give back my stirrups to me, to me,*
> *Sergeant, Sergeant, oh give back my stirrups to me.*

BOMBED LAST NIGHT

Tune: The music hall song *'Drunk Last Night and Drunk the Night Before'*

Bombed last night and bombed the night before,
Going to get bombed tonight if we never get bombed anymore.
When we're bombed, we are scared as we can be.
Can't stop the bombing from old Higher Germany.

CHORUS
They're warning us, they're warning us
One shell hole for the four of us
Thank your lucky stars there is no more of us
'Cos one of us can fill it all alone.

Gassed last night and gassed the night before,
Going to get gassed tonight if we never get gassed anymore.
When we're gassed we're sick as we can be.
For Phosgene and Mustard Gas is much too much for me.

CHORUS
They're killing us, they're killing us
One respirator for the four of us.
Thank your lucky stars there is no more of us
So one of us can take it all alone.

Alternative choruses:
Glorious, victorious,
One bottle of beer between the four of us,
And glory be to God that there isn't any more of us,
For one of us could drink the bleedin' lot

Glorious! Glorious!
One shell hole among the four of us.
Soon there will be no more of us,
Only the bloody old hole.

OLD SOLDIERS NEVER DIE

The sardonic humour and mockingly melancholy tune made this traditional song very popular with the new recruits.

> Old soldiers never die
> Never die,
> Never die;
> Old soldiers never die
> Young ones wish they would.
>
> This rain will never stop,
> Never stop,
> Never stop;
> This rain will never stop
> No, oh! no, no, no.

old soldiers never die, they simply fades a - way

MY LITTLE WET HOLE IN THE TRENCH

Tune: *'My Little Grey Home In The West'*

Written in 1915 by Tom Skeyhill. Though this song describes the sodden conditions in the Flanders trenches it was popular in the Middle East, and published as a pamphlet by the *Egyptian Mail*. 'Jack Johnson's' were heavy artillery shells that gave off a distinctive black smoke, and were named after the heavyweight boxing champion of the world

> I've a little wet hole in a trench,
> Where the rainstorms continually drench;
> There are shell stars that shine,
> Every night just at nine,
> And a lot of things you civvies miss;
> There are whizz-bangs and five-nines galore,
> And the mice and the rats I adore;
> Sure, with a bomb from the air,
> Why, no place can compare,
> With my little wet home in the trench.
>
> There's a little wet home in the trench,
> Where the rain drops continually drench,
> There's a dead cow close by,
> With her feet towards the sky,
> And she gives off a terrible stench.
> Underneath me instead of a floor,
> There's a mass of some mud and some straw,
> And the 'Jack Johnson's' tear,
> Through the rain-sodden air,
> In my little wet home in the trench.

FRED KARNO'S ARMY

Tune: The hymn *'The Church's One Foundation'*

Fred Karno was the leader of of a group of knockabout comedians in a show- stopping act of imbecility and absurd incompetence. Several comedians appeared in his act, including the young Charlie Chaplin; as a member of Karno's Vaudeville company he went to Hollywood in 1914, and graduated into the motion picture business.

This song varied in a few details from unit to unit. Australians and New Zealanders, for example, sang 'ANZAC' for 'ragtime infantry' in the last line. The British used their individual regiment's or unit's names to replace 'ragtime infantry'.

> We are Fred Karno's Army,
> What bloody use are we?
> We cannot fight, we cannot shoot,
> So we joined the infantry,
> But when we get to Berlin,
> The Kaiser he will say,
> 'Hoch! Hoch!! Mein Gott,
> What a jolly fine lot
> Are the ragtime infantry!'
>
> We are Fred Karno's Army,
> A jolly lot are we,
> Fred Karno is our Captain,
> Charlie Chaplin our O.C.
> But when we get to Berlin,
> The Kaiser he will say,
> 'Hoch! Hoch!! Mein Gott,
> What a jolly fine lot
> Are the boys of Company C!'

An Australian version:

> We are the only heroes
> Who stormed the Dardanelles,
> And when we get to Berlin
> They'll say, 'What bloody sells.
> You boast and skive from morn to night
> And think you're very brave,
> But the men who really did the job
> Are dead and in their graves.'

ODE TO CORPORAL

Tune: *'My Bonny lies over the Ocean'*

In some units there was strong resentment towards certain NCOs (Sergeants or Corporals). Here are two examples.

Last night as I lay on my pillow,
Last night as I lay on my bed,
I dreamt our old corp'ral was dying,
I dreamt the old bugger was dead.

CHORUS
Send him,
Oh send him,
Oh send our old corporal to He-e-ll;
Oh keep him,
Oh keep him,
Oh keep the old buffer in Hell.

WE'VE GOT A SERGEANT-MAJOR

We've got a sergeant-major,
Who's never seen a gun;
He's mentioned in despatches
For drinking privates' rum,
And when he sees old Jerry
You should see the bugger run
Miles and miles and miles behind the lines!

THE BELLS OF HELL GO TING-A-LING-A-LING

Tune: 'She Only Answered "Ting-a-ling-a-ling" '

Often sung by soldiers as they came out of the line as others were passing, heading for the Front. Strong emphasis was put on the word 'you'.

> The Bells of Hell go ting-a-ling-a-ling
> For you but not for me:
> For me the angels sing-a-ling-a-ling,
> For *you* but not for me.
>
> Oh! Death, where is they sting-a-ling-a-ling
> Oh! Grave, thy victory?
> The Bells of Hell go ting-a-ling-a-ling
> For *you* but not for me.

WE'RE ALL WAITING FOR A SHELL

Tune: *'We're All Waiting for a Girl'*

The numbers mentioned refer to various calibres of artillery shells; the song reflects the soldiers' longing to receive a minor 'Blighty' wound, so that they can be re-patriated to Britain, and a comfortable hospital.

> We're all waiting for a shell,
> Send us a whizz-bang.
> We're all waiting for a shell,
> Send us a five-nine.
> We don't care whether it's round or square,
> Whether it bursts on the parapet or in the air,
> We're all waiting for a shell,
> Send us a nine-two,
> Please don't keep us waiting long,
> For we want to go to Blighty,
> Where the nurses change our nighties,
> When the right shell comes along.

FRAY MARIE

Tune: *'My Home in Tennessee'*

A song sung by British and Australian soldiers and sailors about a girl in a brothel. 'Framaries' is a French village on the Arras front.

> Way down in Fray Marie
> Ten francs I paid to see
> A French tattooed lady,
> Tattooed from head to knee.
> On her left jaw
> Was the Royal Flying Corps,
> And on her back
> Was the Union Jack.
> Could anyone ask for more?
>
> And up and down her spine
> Are the Coldstream Guards in line,
> And on her shapely hips
> Is a fleet of battleships.
> Tattooed on each kidney
> Is a bird's-eye view of Sydney.
> Around the corner,
> The Johnny Horner,
> My girl from Battersea.

I DON'T WANT TO BE A SOLDIER

Tune: *'Come, My Lad, and Be a Soldier'*

The reference to a 'high-born lady' was a joke understood by the soldiers – the obvious ryhme is 'whore'!

> I don't want to be a soldier,
> I don't want to go to War.
> I'd rather stay at home,
> Around the streets to roam
> And live on the earnings of a high-born lady.
> I don't want a bayonet up my arse-hole,
> I don't want my bollocks shot away,
> I'd rather stay in England,
> Merry, merry England
> And fornicate my bleeding life away.

J·H·DOWD·17

RAINING AND GROUSING

Tune: The hymn '*Holy, Holy, Holy*'

As with so many of the songs of the First World War, this was set to a hymn tune familiar to most soldiers from church services or school assemblies.

> Raining, raining, raining,
> Always bloody well raining.
> Raining all the morning,
> And raining all the night.
>
> Grousing, grousing, grousing,
> Always bloody well grousing.
> Grousing at the rations,
> And grousing at the pay.
>
> Marching, marching, marching,
> Always bloody well marching,
> Marching all the morning
> And marching all the night.
>
> Marching, marching, marching,
> Always bloody well marching;
> Roll on till my time is up
> And I shall march no more.

HANGING ON THE OLD BARBED WIRE

Tune: Traditional

There are many versions of this song which range from the actions of the General down to the long suffering private soldier, but all end with the haunting final line of the last verse: '*I've seen 'em, I've seen 'em, hanging on the old barbed wire.*' Officers sometimes tried to stop the Tommies singing the last verse because it was considered bad for morale; they were usually unsuccessful.

If you want to find the Sergeant,
I know where he is, I know where he is, I know where he is.
If you want to find the Sergeant, I know where he is,
He's lying on the canteen floor.
I've seen him, I've seen him, lying on the canteen floor,
I've seen him, I've seen him, lying on the canteen floor.

If you want to find the Quarter-bloke
I know where he is, I know where he is, I know where he is.
If you want to find the Quarter-bloke, I know where he is,
He's miles and miles behind the line.
I've seen him, I've seen him, miles and miles and miles behind the line.
I've seen him, I've seen him, miles and miles and miles behind the line.

If you want the Sergeant-major,
I know where he is, I know where he is, I know where he is.
If you want the Sergeant-major, I know where he is.
He's tossing off the privates' rum.
I've seen him, I've seen him, tossing off the privates' rum.
I've seen him, I've seen him, tossing off the privates' rum.

If you want the C.O.,
I know where he is, I know where he is, I know where he is.
If you want the C.O., I know where he is
He is down in a deep dug-out
I've seen him, I've seen him, down in a deep dug-out,
I've seen him, I've seen him, down in a deep dug-out.

If you want to find the old battalion,
I know where they are, I know where they are, I know where
  they are.
If you want the old battalion, I know where they are,
They're hanging on the old barbed wire,
I've seen 'em, I've *seen* 'em, hanging on the old barbed wire.
I've seen 'em, I've *seen* 'em, hanging on the old barbed wire.

WASH ME IN THE WATER

Tune: Salvation Army hymn

Said to have been sung by the Regular Army before 1914 but well
known up and down the Western Front throughout 1914–18. A vari-
ant for 'your dirty daughter', when no officers were present, was 'the
Colonel's daughter'. A favourite of the 6th Royal Scots Fusiliers when
Winston Churchill was their Commanding Officer in early 1916.

Whiter than the whitewash on the wall,
Whiter than the whitewash on the wall,
Wash me in the water
That you washed your dirty daughter in
And I shall be whiter
Than the whitewash on the wall, on the wall, on the wall
Whiter than the whitewash on the wall.

FAR, FAR FROM YPRES I LONG TO BE

Tune: *'Sing Me to Sleep'*

'Ypres' is pronounced 'Eepr', but 'Yeeprez' by the Tommies. Adapted from a ballad dating from before 1914, the sentiments are a mixture of longing, stark reality and despair; over half a million men of all nationalities died in the Ypres salient during the war. The names of 55,000 allied soldiers who died with no known grave are inscribed on the Menin Gate at Ypres.

Sing me to sleep where bullets fall,
Let me forget the war and all;
Damp is my dug-out, cold are my feet,
Nothing but bully and biscuits to eat.
Over the sandbags, helmets you'll find
Corpses in front and corpses behind.

CHORUS
Far, far from Ypre-es I long to be,
Where German snipers can't get at me,
Damp is my dug-out, cold are my feet,
Waiting for whizz-bangs to send me to sleep.

Sing me to sleep in some old shed,
The rats all running around my head,
Stretched out upon my waterproof,
Dodging the raindrops through the roof,
Dreaming of home and nights in the West,
Somebody's oversized boots on my chest.

CHORUS
Far, far from Ypre-es I long to be, (etc.)

HUSH! HERE COMES A WHIZZ-BANG

Tune: *'Hush! Here Comes the Dream Man'*

The song was sung by the troops in *estaminets* as a gesture of defiance. If you made a joke of the prospects of death, it would not happen to you. A whizz-bang was a German shell. The word 'bang!' in the final line was shouted out by the soldiers.

Hush! Here comes a whizz-bang,
Hush! Here comes a whizz-bang,
Now then soldier, get down them stairs,
Into your dug-out and say your prayers.
Hush! Here comes a whizz-bang,
And it's making straight for you:
And you'll see all the wonders of No Man's Land
If a whizz-bang (BANG!) gets you.

I WANT TO GO HOME

Written in 1915 by Gitz Rice

In a letter home after his first action in June 1916, the poet and composer Ivor Gurney who volunteered for the 2nd/5th Gloucesters wrote: '"*I want to go home*" is a song our men sang when the last strafe was at its hottest – a very popular song about here; but not at all military… Not a brave song, but brave men sing it.'

William Cushing of the 9th Norfolk Regiment was to recall to Lyn Macdonald: 'I remember one night, the night was still and silent, when someone started to sing *sotto voce* that haunting, nostalgic cry, taken up by all: "Oh my, I don't want to die. I want to go home." I can still hear that murmured wish and longing.'

I want to go home,
I want to go home,
I don't want to go in the trenches no more,
Where the whizz-bangs and shrapnel they whistle and roar
Take me over the sea
Where the Alleyman can't get at me.
Oh my,
I don't want to die,
I want to go home.

I want to go home,
I want to go home,
I don't want to visit la Belle France no more,
For oh the Jack Johnsons they make such a roar.
Take me over the sea
Where the snipers they can't snipe at me.
Oh my,
I don't want to die,
I want to go home.

IF YOU WERE THE ONLY BOCHE IN THE TRENCH

Tune: '*If You Were the Only Girl in the World*'
Written by Clifford Grey and Nat D. Ayer

The original version was sung by Violet Loraine and Georges Robey in the hugely popular revue '*The Bing Boys*', which ran throughout the war. It quickly became a hit in France, brought out in the form of gramophone records or sheet music by soldiers returning from leave.

The original song:

> *If you were the only girl in the world,*
> *And I was the only boy,*
> *Nothing else would matter in the world today,*
> *We would go on loving in the same old way.*
> *A Garden of Eden just made for two,*
> *With nothing to mar our joy,*
> *There would be such wonderful things to do,*
> *I would say such wonderful things to you,*
> *If you were the only girl in the world,*
> *And I was the only boy.*

The Tommies' version:

> If you were the only Boche in the trench,
> And I had the only bomb,
> Nothing else would matter in the world today,
> I would blow you in to eternity.
> Chamber of Horrors, just made for two,
> With nothing to spoil our fun;
> There would be such a heap of things to do,
> I should get your rifle and bayonet too,
> If you were the only Boche in the trench,
> And I had the only gun.

IF THE SERGEANT STEALS YOUR RUM

Tune: *'Though Your Heart May Ache a While, Never Mind'*

Here is an example of how soldiers appropriated the chorus of a sentimental song of 1913 by Harry Dent and Tom Goldburn.

The original song:

> *Though your heart may ache awhile,*
> *Never mind!*
> *Though your face may lose its smile,*
> *Never mind!*
> *For there's sunshine after rain,*
> *And then gladness follows pain.*
> *You'll be happy once again,*
> *Never mind.*

The parody:

> If the sergeant steals your rum,
> Never mind!
> If the sergeant steals your rum,
> Never mind!
> Though he's just a bloody sot,
> Just let him take the lot,
> If the sergeant steals your rum,
> Never mind!
>
> If old Jerry shells the trench,
> Never mind!
> If old Jerry shells the trench,
> Never mind!
> Though the blasted sandbags fly
> You have only once to die,
> If old Jerry shells the trench,
> Never mind!

If you get stuck on the wire,
Never mind!
If you get stuck on the wire,
Never mind!
Though the light's as broad as day
When you die they stop your pay,
If you get stuck on the wire,
Never mind!

I WORE A TUNIC

Tune: '*I Wore a Tulip*'

A song sung by the the veterans of Kitchener's Army about the conscripts, who came out in 1917.

The Battle of Loos in September 1915 was the first in which a significant number of the newly trained Kitchener's Army battalions were engaged and by 1917, after the Somme, they were hardened veterans.

I wore a tunic,
An old khaki tunic,
While you wore your civvie clothes.
We fought and bled at Loos
While you were on the booze,
The booze no one here knows.
You were with the wenches
While we were in the trenches
Facing the German foe.
Oh, you were a-slacking
While we were attacking
The Boche up the Menin Road.

MADEMOISELLE FROM ARMENTEERS

Armenti`eres – the 'Armenteers' of the troops, a few miles behind the front line – was a centre of rest and relaxation for men coming out of the trenches.

> Mademoiselle from Armenteers, parlay-voo,
> Mademoiselle from Armenteers, parlay-voo,
> Mademoiselle from Armenteers,
> She hasn't been kissed for forty years,
> Hinky pinky, parlay-voo.
>
> Our top kick in Armenteers, parlay-voo,
> Our top kick in Armenteers, parlay-voo,
> Our top kick in Armenteers
> Soon broke the spell of forty years,
> Hinky pinky, parlay-voo.
>
> The officers get all the steak, parlay-voo,
> The officers get all the steak, parlay-voo,
> The officers get all the steak
> And all we get is a belly ache,
> Hinky pinky, parlay-voo.
>
> From gay Paree we heard guns roar, parlay-voo,
> From gay Paree we heard guns roar, parlay-voo,
> From gay Paree we heard guns roar,
> But all we heard was 'Je t'adore',
> Hinky pinky, parlay-voo.
>
> You might forget the gas and shell, parlay-voo,
> You might forget the gas and shell, parlay-voo,
> You might forget the gas and shell,
> You'll never forget the mademoiselle,
> Hinky pinky, parlay-voo.

FARMER HAVE YOU ANY GOOD WINE?

Tune: *'Mademoiselle from Armenteers'*

It is believed that there are over sixty different versions of this song, varying from the polite to the grossly obscene. All of them however were sung with enthusiasm. This is a version sung by soldiers of the 13th Battalion of the Rifle Brigade.

Farmer have you any good wine, parlez vous
Farmer have you any good wine, parlez vous
Farmer have you any good wine, fit for a soldier up the line,
Inky pinky parlez vous.
Yes, I have some very good wine, parlez vous
Oh yes, I have some very good wine, parlez vous
Oh yes, I have some very good wine, fit for a soldier up the line,
Inky pinky parlez vous.

Oh farmer have you a daughter fine, parlez vous
Oh farmer have you a daughter fine, parlez vous
Oh farmer have you a daughter fine, fit for a soldier up the line,
Inky pinky parlez vous.

Yes, I have a daughter fine, parlez vous
Oh yes, I have a daughter fine, parlez vous
Oh yes, I have a daughter fine, fit for a soldier up the line,
Inky pinky parlez vous.

Then up the stairs and into bed, parlez vous
And up the stairs and into bed, parlez vous
And up the stairs and into bed, we'll shag her till her cheeks are
  red,
Inky pinky parlez vous.

NEUVE CHAPELLE

Tune: *'The Rambling Irishman'*

The village of Neuve Chapelle is situated to the south-west of Lille. British and Indian soldiers took the village in March 1915 but with heavy casualties, including men of the 2nd Royal Irish Rifles and 1st Leinster who were part of the 27th Division. It was a sergeant of this division who composed this song, which became a favourite of the Irish. Although they did not succeed in attaining their furthest objectives, it was the first successful engagement in the first major battle of 1915.

For when we landed in Belgium the girls all danced with joy;
Says one unto the other, 'Here comes an Irish Boy.'
Then it's fare thee well, dear mother, we'll do the best we can,
For you know that Neuve Chapelle was won by an Irishman.

CHORUS
Then here's good luck to the Rifles, the Inniskillings, too;
The Royal Irish Fusiliers and the Royal Artillery, too;
For side by side they fought and died as noble heroes can,
And you all know well that Neuve Chapelle was won by an
Irishman.

Said von Kluck unto the Kaiser, 'What are we going to do?
We're going to meet those Irishmen, and the men we never knew.'
Says the Kaiser unto old von Kluck, 'We'll do the best we can,
But I'm telling you true that Waterloo was won by an Irishman.'

CHORUS
Then here's good luck to the Rifles, the Inniskillings, too; (etc.)

General von Kluck was the commander of the German forces; his fortuitous name happily rhymed with the Tommies' favourite swear word.

How Sergeant O'Leary of the Irish Guards Won the V.C.

DRAWN BY F. MATANIA, MARCH, 1915

SERGEANT O'LEARY, V.C., ATTACKING THE GERMAN MACHINE-GUN CREW SINGLE-HANDED

THE OLD FRENCH TRENCH

This song was heard by Lyn Macdonald when sung by Bert Lister, who had served in the 12th Battalion the Rifle Brigade, and was passionately fond of concert parties. Most divisions had permanent concert parties which moved around with the troops. The 37th Division concert party was 'The Barn Owls', and that of the 20th Division to which Bert Lister belonged, was 'The Verey Lights'. It was started and run by Captain A. Gilbey, who was a gifted musician and knew what the soldiers liked. He wrote '*The Old French Trench*' in 1915 and it regularly brought the house down.

When you're living in the trenches where we've been,
The Boche may be heard but he's seldom seen.
You go on patrol in a dickens of a funk,
You lie in the hole that a sailor's sunk.
You think up a tale to tell the boss,
You reckon you deserve the Military Cross.
You say that you cut the old barbed wire,
Everybody says you're a bloody liar.

CHORUS
Oh what a life, living in a trench,
Oh what a life, fighting with the French.
We haven't got a wife or a pretty little wench,
But everybody's happy in the old French trench.

Everybody's happy, everybody's glad,
It's the seventeenth bloody shell we've had.
Whizz-bang coalbox shrapnel-soar,
And a blinking mine underneath the floor.

CHORUS
Oh what a life, living in a trench, (etc.)

THEY WERE ONLY PLAYING LEAP-FROG

Tune: '*John Brown's Body*'

This was a song sung by young subalterns, not by Tommies. It was the junior officers who suffered most from staff officers.

One grasshopper jumped right over another grasshopper's back,
And another grasshopper jumped right over that other grasshopper's back,
A third grasshopper jumped right over the two grasshoppers'
  backs,
And a fourth grasshopper jumped right over all the other
  grasshoppers' backs.

CHORUS
They were only playing leap-frog,
They were only playing leap-frog,
They were only playing leap-frog,
When one staff officer jumped right over
The other staff officer's back.

One staff officer jumped right over
  another staff officer's back,
And another staff officer jumped right
  over that other staff officers' back,
A third staff officer jumped right over
  the two staff officers' backs,
And a fourth staff officer jumped right
  over all the other staff officers' backs.

THE ASC TO THE WAR HAVE GONE

Tune: *'The Minstrel Boy'*

Sung by the front line troops who did not have much respect for the ASC, the Army Service Corps, though they carried out an often dangerous job.

'Maconochie' is the maker's name of tinned stew consisting mainly of sliced vegetables, chiefly turnips and carrots in a thin soup. Warmed in the tin or eaten cold it was initially a welcome change from bully beef.

The ASC to the war have gone,
At the base at Havre you will find them,
Their shining spurs they have girded on,
But they have left their bayonets behind them.
'What's the sense,' cried the ASC,
'Of taking to France the damn things?
Their only use, it seems to me,
Is to open the Tommy's jam tins.'

The ASC were driving by
When a German shell came over.
At once, determined to do or die,
They one and all took cover.
Their letters home described that shell,
And the guns the Huns turned on them.
They did not mention that the pip-squeak fell
At least a mile beyond them.

But thank the Lord for ASC,
The pride and joy of the nation,
Who bring our bully and jam and tea,
And our Maconochie ration.
Here's good luck to the ASC,
Though if they'd never come, boys,
I bet we'd get all the strawberry,
Instead of apple and plum, boys.

PLUM AND APPLE

Tune: *'A Wee Deoch an' Doris'*

'Plum and Apple' was the only kind of jam which reached the fighting troops and was much mocked in song. Here are two examples.

> Plum and Apple,
> Apple and Plum,
> Plum and Apple,
> Apple and Plum,
> There is always some.
> The A.S.C. get strawberry jam
> And lashings of rum.
> But we poor blokes
> We only get –
> Apple and Plum.

TICKLER'S JAM

Tune: *'Any Old Iron'*

Tickler's was the brand of jam supplied to the troops in the early war years.

> Tickler's jam, Tickler's jam, how I love Tickler's jam.
> Plum and apple in a one-pound pot,
> Sent from Blighty in a ten-ton lot.
> Every night when I'm asleep I'm dreaming that I am
> Forcing my way through the Dardanelles with a ton of Tickler's
> jam.

WHEN VERY LIGHTS ARE SHINING

Tune: '*When Irish Eyes Are Smiling*'
Original tune written by George Graff and Chauncey Olcott in 1913

A 'Very light' is a rocket fired from a brass pistol, and used at night in the front-line to illuminate No Man's Land so that sentries could be sure the enemy were not approaching. Also used for signalling that a position had been captured, or for help in an emergency.

On occasion the Very light floated slowly and menacingly down attached to a small parachute, during which time no-one in open ground dare move.

When Very lights are shining,
Sure they're like the morning light
And when the guns begin to thunder
You can hear the angel's shite.
Then the Maxims start to chatter
And trench mortars send a few,
And when Very lights are shining
'Tis time for a rum issue.

When Very lights are shining
Sure 'tis like the morning dew,
And when shells begin a bursting
It makes you think your time's come
   too.
And when you start advancing
Five nines and gas comes through,
Sure when Very lights are shining
'Tis rum or lead for you.

HERE'S TO THE GOOD OLD BEER

This traditional marching song was sung with gusto evoking memories of nights back home in pubs: beer in France was scarce and weak compared with British beer. Rum was issued to the soldiers every night in the line.

Here's to the good old beer,
Mop it down, mop it down!
Here's to the good old beer,
Mop it down, mop it down!
Here's to the good old beer
That never leaves you queer,
Here's to the good old beer,
Mop it down!

Here's to the good old stout — that makes you care for nowt.
Here's to the good old porter — that slips down as it oughter.
Here's to the good old whiskey — the stuff that makes you frisky.
Here's to the good old port — that makes you feel a sport.
Here's to the good old brandy — the stuff that makes you randy.
Here's to the good old rum — that warms your balls and bum.

Here's to the good old gin,
Mop it down, mop it down!
Here's to the good old gin,
Mop it down!
Here's to the good old gin
That fills you up with sin,
Here's to the good old gin,
Mop it down!

APRÈS LA GUERRE FINI

Tune: '*Sous les Ponts de Paris*' (Under the Bridges of Paris)

A parody of '*Sous les Ponts de Paris*' which was a popular song in France in 1916. The Tommies' version was sung in *estaminets* when the *vin blanc* was flowing freely; this is one of many.

Après la guerre fini,
Soldat Anglais parti;
Mam'selle Fransay boko pleuray
Après la guerre fini.

Après la guerre fini,
Soldat Anglais parti,
Mademoiselle in the family way,
Après la guerre fini

Après la guerre fini,
Soldat anglais parti;
Mademoiselle can go to hell
Après la guerre fini.

DO YOUR BALLS HANG LOW?

Lyn Macdonald in her book, *Somme*, recalls Sir Douglas Haig, the Commander-in-Chief overhearing this song being sung by a battalion marching by an HQ that he was visiting. He immediately mounted his horse and set off in pursuit of the battalion commander. When he came alongside him he found he was singing as heartily as the rest of his men, so heartily in fact that he had failed to notice the falling off of the merry chorus behind him and was bawling in a rousing oblivious crescendo '*Can you sling them on your shoulder, like a lousy fucking soldier? Do your balls hang low?*' Haig congratulated him on his fine voice, but added: 'But you must know that in any circumstances these words are inexcusable.'

As soon as Haig was out of earshot one wag started up the song: '*After the ball is over…*'

> Do your balls hang low?
> Do they dangle to and fro?
> Can I tie them in a knot?
> Can you tie them in a bow?
>
> Do they itch when it's hot?
> Do you rest them in a pot?
>
> Do you get them in a tangle?
> Do you catch them in a mangle?
> Do they swing in stormy weather?
> Do they tickle with a feather?
>
> Do they rattle when you walk?
> Do they jingle when you talk?
>
> Can you sling them on your shoulder
> Like a lousy fucking soldier?
> DO YOUR BALLS HANG LOW?

THAT SHIT SHUTE

Tune: *'Wrap me Up in my Tarpaulin Jacket'*

Cameron Shute was a British Army General who could not come to terms with the peculiar ways of the Royal Naval Division, and he resolved to shape them up. In doing so he alienated his men who did not share his obsession with cleanliness. This parody was composed by A.P. Herbert who was an officer in his division. Herbert later went on to become a well-known writer and dramatist.

> The General inspecting the trenches
> Exclaimed with a horrified shout,
> 'I refuse to command a Division
> Which leaves its excreta about.'
>
> But nobody took any notice
> No one was prepared to refute,
> That the presence of shit was congenial
> Compared to the presence of Shute.
>
> And certain responsible critics
> Made haste to reply to his words
> Observing that his Staff advisers
> Consisted entirely of turds.
>
> For shit may be shot at odd corners
> And paper supplied there to suit,
> But a shit would be shot without mourners
> If somebody shot that shit Shute.

WE ARE BUT LITTLE SEAFORTHS WEAK

Tune: The Methodist hymn *'We Are But Little Children Weak'*

'The Seaforths' are the Seaforth Highlanders, who like most infantry regiments complained of low pay and lack of leave.

> We are but little Seaforths weak,
> Our pay is seven bob a week.
> Whate'er we do by night or day,
> It makes no difference to our pay.
>
> Our hours a day are twenty-four.
> We thank the lord there are no more,
> For if there were we know that we
> Would work another two or three.
>
> There is one thing we do believe,
> That we're entitled to some leave.
> We know not why we are so cursed,
> We'll get our old-age pensions first.

GILLYMONG

Tune: *'Moonlight Bay'*, written by Percy Wenrich and Edward Madden, 1912

At the start of the Somme offensive in July 1916 there was sustained fighting in the Guillemont ('Gillymong') area and trenches were taken and re-taken.

We were rushing along
In Gillymong:
We could hear the Boche a singing:
They seemed to say,
'You have stolen our trench,
But don't go away,
And we'll pepper you with tear shells
All the day.'

We were waiting for them
Later on in the day;
You might have heard our voices singing:
'Don't lose your way.
This is your old trench,
Now, do step this way,
And we'll give you souvenirs
To take away.'

A verse invented by Rifleman Stevens, 10 Battalion, The Kings Royal Rifle Corps.

I was strolling along in Gillymong –
With the Minniewerfers singing
Their old sweet song
And I said to old Fritz,
'We're here to stay!
And we'll kick your arse from here
To Moonlight Bay.'

THEY DIDN'T BELIEVE ME

Written in 1914 by M. E. Rourke and composed by Jerome Kern

The original song:

> *And when I told them*
> *How beautiful you are*
> *They didn't believe me!*
> *They didn't believe me!*
> *You lips, your eyes, your cheeks, your hair*
> *Are in a class beyond compare*
> *You're the loveliest girl that one could see!*
>
> *And when I tell them*
> *And I'm certainly going to tell them,*
> *That I'm the man whose wife one day you'll be,*
> *They'll never believe me,*
> *They'll never believe me,*
> *That from this great big world you've chosen me!*

The parody is particularly powerful:

> And when they asked us
> How dangerous it was.
> Oh! We'll never tell them,
> No, we'll never tell them.
> We spent our pay in some café,
> And fought wild women night and day,
> T'was the cushiest job we ever had.
>
> And when they ask us,
> And they're certainly going to ask us.
> The reason why we didn't win the
> Croix de Guerre.
> Oh! We'll never tell them,
> No! We'll never tell them.
> There was a front but damned if we knew where.

HIGH WOOD TO WATERLOT FARM

Tune: *'Chalk Farm to Camberwell Green'*
From the popular musical *Bric-a-Brac*, produced in 1915 at the Palace
Theatre, London

Chalk Farm to Camberwell Green referred to the longest bus ride which could be had for a penny, and was a popular Sunday afternoon outing for courting couples.

High Wood and Waterlot Farm were fought for at terrible cost in July 1916 at the start of the Battle of the Somme. The parody was written by Lieutenant Ewart MackIntosh, 4th Seaforth Highlanders, who was wounded and gassed at High Wood; he was killed at the battle of Cambrai in November 1917.

Original words:

> *Chalk Farm to Camberwell Green*
> *All on a summer's day.*
> *Up you get to the top of the bus*
> *And you're spooning all the way.*
> *When we got to the end of the ride,*
> *He asked me to go for a walk,*
> *But I'm not so Camberwell Green*
> *By a very long chalk.*

Parody:

> There is a wood at the top of the hill,
> If it's not shifted it's standing there still;
> There is a farm a short distance away,
> But I'd not advise you to go there by day,
> For the snipers abound, and the shells are not rare,
> And a man's only chance is to run like a hare,
> So take my advice if you're chancing your arm
> From High Wood to Waterlot Farm.

CHORUS
High Wood to Waterlot Farm,
All on a summer's day,
Up you get to the top of the trench
Though you're sniped at all the way.
If you've got a smoke helmet there
You'd best put it on if you could,
For the wood down by Waterlot Farm
Is a bloody high wood.

THE WATCH ON THE RHINE

Written by E.W. Mark and Herman Darewski

In her book *To the Last Man: Spring 1918*, Lyn Macdonald describes the last defiant gesture of C295 Battery on the Third Army front, before they were overrun by the Germans in March 1918. The Battery Commander, Captain Parrish, before leaving the dugout hurriedly, left this song (sung by Harry Tate and Violet Loraine) on the gramophone for the Germans to hear when they arrived. Lieutenant Ernst Junger, who understood English and had just lost four of his men, wound up the gramophone and was so infuriated by the words of the song that he sent the gramophone crashing to the floor! Junger described his reactions in his own book *Storm of Steel* (1929).

When we've wound up the Watch on the Rhine,
How we'll sing 'Auld Land Syne'!
You and I 'Hoorah!' we'll cry,
Everything will be Potsdam fine.
When we've wound up the Watch on the Rhine,
Then they won't have the option of fine,

Since to jail they'll be lugged,
All the Herrs will be jugged,
When we've wound up the Watch on the Rhine.

When we've wound up the Watch on the Rhine,
How we'll sing 'Auld Lang Syne'!
You and I 'Hoorah!' we'll cry,
Everything will be Potsdam fine.
When we've wound up the Watch on the Rhine,
The half-a-Crown Prince must resign,
For instead of the loot, he'll be getting the boot,
When we've wound up the Watch on the Rhine.

WHEN THIS BLOODY WAR IS OVER

Tune: The hymn 'What a Friend We Have in Jesus'

This song originated in the American Civil War where it was called 'When this Lousy War is Over'. An easy tune that lent itself to an infinite number of verses. After the First War, 'bloody' was usually changed to 'rotten' or 'ruddy' in the published versions of the song; but 'bloody' is what the soldiers sang.

> When this bloody war is over,
> No more soldiering for me.
> When I get my civvy clothes on,
> Oh, how happy I shall be!
> No more church parades on Sunday,
> No more putting in for leave,
> I shall kiss the Sergeant-Major
> How I'll miss him; how he'll grieve.

Sometimes the last four lines of this verse were sung as:

> No more going in the trenches,
> No more asking for a pass
> You can tell the Sergeant-Major
> To stick his passes up his arse.

Or:

> I shall sound my own reveille,
> I shall make my own tattoo:
> No more NCOs to curse me,
> No more bloody Army stew.

When this bloody war is over
Guards' fatigues will be no more
We'll be spooning with the wenches
As we did in days of yore.
NCOs will then be navvies,
Privates own their motor cars,
No more 'sirring' and saluting,
No more tea dished out in jars.

GALLIPOLI AND THE ANZACS

"The Australian and New Zealand troops have indeed
proved themselves worthy sons of the Empire."

GEORGE R.I.

OLD GALLIPOLI'S A WONDERFUL PLACE

Tune: *'Mountains of Mourne'*

For the British, Australian and New Zealand troops, there was little time, leisure, or opportunity in the conditions of the peninsula of Gallipoli for concerts – no *estaminets*, no canteens, no towns, no civilians. The only respite from the trenches was the fly-ridden dugouts, the narrow sandy beaches, and occasionally a swim in the waters of the Aegean with a constant risk of being shelled. In the raging heat of the summer even the despised and thirst-inducing bully-beef would turn to liquid mush in the tins. Unsurprisingly, in one of the rare songs which can be attributed to the soldiers in Gallipoli their thoughts focused on food. The hill of Achi Baba was never captured, and Gallipoli was evacuated in January 1916, nine months after the original landing.

> Oh, old Gallipoli's a wonderful place,
> Where the boys in the trenches the foe have to face,
> But they never grumble, they smile through it all,
> Very soon they expect Achi Baba to fall.
> At least when I asked them, that's what they told me
> In Constantinople quite soon we would be,
> But if war lasts till Doomsday I think we'll still be
> Where old Gallipoli sweeps down to the sea.
>
> We don't grow potatoes or barley or wheat,
> So we're aye on the lookout for something to eat,
> We're fed up with biscuits and bully and ham
> And we're sick of the sight of yon parapet jam.
> Send out steak and onions and nice ham and eggs
> And a fine big fat chicken with five or six legs,
> And a drink of the stuff that begins with a 'B'
> Where the old Gallipoli sweeps down to the sea.

SUVLA BAY

Written by Jack Spode

This song about Gallipoli was popular in Australia, even though there were no Australian forces at Suvla Bay, where the Allies launched an attack on 10 August 1915. The Australians and New Zealanders fought together at Gallipoli as the ANZACs.

In an old Australian homestead
With the roses round the door
A girl received a letter
From a far and distant shore.
With her mother's arms around her
'Neath the blue Australian skies:
She slowly read the letter
And tears fell from her eyes.

CHORUS
Why do I weep
Why do I pray
My love's asleep so far away.
He played his part
That August day
And left my heart
On Suvla Bay.

Then she joined a band of sisters
Beneath a cross of red,
Just to try to do her duty
To her sweetheart who lay dead.
Many fellows came to woo her
But were sadly turned away
When she told them the sad,
Sad story of her love
On Suvla Bay.

MADEMOISELLE FROM ARMENTEERS

Tune: *'Mademoiselle From Armenteers'*

An Australian (and surpisingly mild!) version of the bawdy song sung so enthusiastically by the Tommies.

> Mademoiselle from Armenteers, parlez-vous,
> Sang the diggers between their beers, parlez-vous,
> And soldier's chorus and ballad gay,
> Rang through the old estaminet,
> Inky pinky parlez-vous.

Men from Wagga and Gundagai, parlez-vous,
From Perth, the Towers and Boggabri, parlez-vous,
From Sydney city and Dandenong,
Sinking their sorrows in wine and song,
Inky pinky parlez-vous.

Mademoiselle enjoyed the din, parlez-vous,
She tripped around with the bock and the vin, parlez-vous,
And Mademoiselle in an innocent way,
Trolled a stave of a ribald lay,
Inky pinky parlez-vous.

One young digger, tanned and lean, parlez-vous,
From Darling Downs or the Riverine, parlez-vous,
Set her heart in a rapturous whirl,
When he vowed that she was his dinkum girl,
Inky pinky parlez-vous.

They laughed and loved in that old French town, parlez-vous,
And her heart spoke out of those eyes of brown, parlez-vous,
But the time went by and there came the day,
When he and his cobbers all marched away,
Inky pinky parlez-vous.

Maybe on a field in France he fell, parlez-vous,
No word came back to Mademoiselle, parlez-vous,
But a little French girl with eyes of brown,
Prayed for him still in that war-swept town,
Inky pinky parlez-vous.

Now quiet the old estaminet, parlez-vous,
No more diggers will come this way, parlez-vous,
May your heart grow lighter with passing years,
O Mademoiselle from Armenteers,
Inky pinky parlez-vous.

COME INTO THE LIGHTER

Tune: *'Come Into the Garden, Maude'*
Composed by Michael W. Balfe from the original poem by Tennyson

The original song, which was frequently inflicted on peacetime audiences, was parodied at concert parties after the evacuation of Gallipoli in December 1915 and January 1916. It was inspired by the actions of General Sir Stanley Maude, who refused to leave the beach until he had been re-united with his servant and his baggage – both of which he had apparently mislaid! He was later in command in Mesopotamia against the Turks and captured Baghdad in 1917. He died in the same year of cholera, having refused to be inoculated.

Come into the lighter Maude
The fuse has long been lit,
Come into the lighter Maude,
And never mind your kit.
The waves grow high,
But what care I,
I'd rather be seasick,
Than blown sky-high.
So, come into the lighter Maude,
Or I'm off in the launch alone!

TAKE ME BACK TO DEAR OLD AUSSIE

Tune: '*Take Me Back to Dear Old Blighty*'

Take me back to dear old Aussie,
Put me on the boat for Woolloomooloo;
Take me over there, drop me anywhere,
Sydney, Melbourne, Adelaide, for I don't care;
I just want to see my best girl,
Cuddling up again we soon will be;
Oh, Blighty is a failure, take me back to Australia,
Aussie is the place for me.

WHO KILLED BILL KAISER?

Tune: '*Who Killed Cock Robin?*'

The words 'Chidley' and 'Tidley' are parts of Australian word usage
and folklore. 'Chidley' was a fabricated character who was tradition-
ally blamed for all things that go wrong. 'Tidley' appears to be derived
from the word 'tiddly', i.e. getting drunk.

Who killed Bill Kaiser?
We said the Allies,
Upon the road to Calais,
We killed Bill Kaiser.

CHORUS
Then all of the Germans
Got a great big surpriser,

When they heard of the death of old
Bill Kaiser,
When they heard of the death of poor
Old Bill Kaiser.

Who saw him die?
I did said France,
When they stopped his advance,
I saw him die.

CHORUS
Now the Russians and the Belgians
and British are much wiser,
Since France saw the death of old
Bill Kaiser,
Since France saw the death of poor
Old Bill Kaiser.

Who'll dig his grave?
I will said Chidley,
I'll get on the tidley,
And I'll dig his grave.

CHORUS
Then all the German wowsers vowed
Chidley would rue it,
He said, you made me dig his grave
and I didn't want to do it,
And they put a load of sand on poor
Old Bill Kaiser.

THE DIGGER'S SONG

Tune: V. Hawkins and his Dinah

The popularity of this song, among the Australian troops throughout the war, was undoubtedly an expression of their dislike of staff officers, in particular, and authority in general.

He came up to London and straightway he strode
To the army headquarters in Horseferry Road,
To see all the bludgers who dodge all the strafe
By getting soft jobs on the headquarters staff.

CHORUS
Dinky-die, dinky-die,
I am an old digger and can't tell a lie.

A Buckshee lance-corporal said, 'Pardon me, please.
There's blood on your tunic, there's mud on your sleeve.
You look so disgraceful that people will laugh,'
Said the cold-footed coward on the headquarters staff.

CHORUS
Dinky-die, dinky-die,
I am an old digger and can't tell a lie.

The digger jumped with a murderous glance;
Said, 'I just come from the trenches in France,
Where fighting was plenty and comforts was few,
Brave men were dying for bastards like you.'

CHORUS
Dinky-die, dinky-die,
I am an old digger and can't tell a lie.

'We're shelled on the left and we're shelled on the right.
We're bombed all the day and we're bombed all the night.
If something don't happen, and that pretty soon,
There'll be nobody left in the bloody platoon.'

CHORUS
Dinky-die, dinky-die,
I am an old digger and can't tell a lie.

'Bludgers' are those who sought soft jobs at home. The term 'digger' is believed to have derived from the goldfields in Australia when the word was used to distinguish the holder of mining rights from a 'squatter' or farmer.

SONGS OF THE ROYAL FLYING CORPS

THE DYING AVIATOR

Tune: *'The Tarpaulin Jacket'*

This is the oldest Royal Flying Corps (RFC) song of all; it goes back to 1912 when the Corps was formed from the Balloon Section of the Royal Engineers. It was sung in all the squadron messes during the war.

Oh, the bold aviator lay dying,
And as 'neath the wreckage he lay, he lay,
To the sobbing mechanics about him,
These last dying words he did say:

CHORUS
Two valve springs you'll find in my stomach,
Three spark plugs are safe in my lung
The prop is in splinters inside me,
To my fingers the joy-stick has clung.

Oh, had I the wings of a little dove,
Far a-way, far a-way would I fly, I fly,
Straight to the arms of my true love,
And there would I lay me and die.

CHORUS
Take the propeller boss out of my liver,
Take the aileron out of my thigh, my thigh
From the seat of my pants take the piston,
Then see if the old crate will fly.

Then get you two little white tombstones,
Put them one at my head and my toe, my toe,
And get you a pen-knife and scratch there,
'Here lies a poor pilot below'.

CHORUS
Take the cylinders out of my kidneys,
The connecting rod out of my brain, my brain,
From the small of my back get the crankshaft,
And assemble the engine again.

And get you six brandies and sodas,
And lay them out in a row,
And get you six other good airmen,
To drink to this pilot below. Oh —

CHORUS
Take the cylinders out of my kidneys, (etc.)

And when at the Court of Enquiry
They ask for the reason I died, I died,
Please say I forgot twice iota
Was the minimum angle of glide. Oh —

CHORUS
Take the cylinders out of my kidneys, (etc.)

And when I join the Air Force
Way, way up in the sky, the sky,
Let's hope that they know twice iota
Is the minimum angle to fly. Oh —

CHORUS
Take the cylinders out of my kidneys, (etc.)

Aileron: lateral control-flaps at rear of aircraft wing tips which enable
it to bank either side.

VOCAL NUMBE

WHAT DO YOU WANT T
THOSE EYES AT ME

FROM SOMEONE IN FR
SOMEONE IN SOMER

TOMMY

SHE'S VENUS DE MILO

THE IRISH GIRLS ARE T

DUSTING

I'M SICK OF THIS 'ERE 1
WAR

WASHING

MY WORD! AIN'T WE CA
ON

I WISH I WAS IN BLIGH

Price 2/- Net Each Ne

'ullo!

Bruce Bairnsfather

CHARLES B. COCHRAN'S
PRODUCTION

The Better 'Ole

OR THE ROMANCE OF "OLD BILL"

BY BRUCE BAIRNSFATHER & ARTHUR ELIOT

WHAT DID YOU WANT TO HAVE A CRASH LIKE THAT FOR?

Tune: *'What Do You Want to Make Those Eyes at Me For?'*

A popular Royal Flying Corps song; the original song was from the 1916 revue 'A Better 'Ole' based on the war artist Bruce Bairnsfather's famous character, Old Bill.

> What did you want to have a crash like that for?
> It's the sixth you've had today.
> It makes you sad, it makes me mad,
> It's lucky it was an Avro, not a brand new Spad.
> What did you want to have a crash like that for?
> You'd better clear the wreckage all away,
> But never mind, you'll go up again tonight
> With umpteen bombs all loaded with dynamite,
> And if you have another crash like that one,
> It's the LAST you'll have today.

'Avro': a two-seater bomber.
'Spad': a single-seater fighter aircraft.

WE ARE THE RAGTIME FLYING CORPS

We are the Ragtime Flying Corps,
We are the ragtime boys,
We are respected by every nation,
And we're loved by all the girls (I don't think).
People, they think we're millionaires,
Think we're dealers in stocks and shares;
When we go out all the people roar,
We are the Ragtime Flying Corps.

We are the Ragtime Flying Corps,
We are the R.F.C.
We spend our tanners, we know our manners,
And are respected wherever we go.
Walking up and down the Farnborough Road,
Doors and windows open wide.
We are the boys of the R.F.C.
We don't care a damn for Germany;
We are the Flying Corps.

WE HAVEN'T GOT A HOPE IN THE MORNING

Tune: '*John Peel*'

When you soar into the air on a Sopwith Scout,
And you're scrapping with a Hun and your gun cuts out,
Well, you stuff down your nose till your plugs fall out,
'Cos you haven't got a hope in the morning.

CHORUS
For a batman woke me from my bed,
I'd had a thick night and a very sore head,
And I said to myself, to myself I said,
'Oh, we haven't got a hope in the morning!'

So I went to the sheds and examined my gun,
Then my engine I tried to run;
And the revs. that it gave were a thousand and one,
'Cos it hadn't got a hope in the morning.

CHORUS
For a batman woke me from my bed, (etc.)

We were escorting Twenty-Two,
Hadn't a notion what to do,
So we shot down a Hun and an F.E. too,
'Cos it hadn't got a hope in the morning!

CHORUS
For a batman woke me from my bed, (etc.)

We went to Cambrai, all in vain,
The F.E.s said, 'We must explain;
Our camera's broke; we must do it again;
Oh, we haven't got a hope tomorrow morning.'

NOW I'M A GENERAL AT THE MINISTRY

A parody of '*I am the Ruler of the Queen's Navee*', from Gilbert and Sullivan's *HMS Pinafore*. Sung towards the end of 1918.

When I was a boy I went to war
As an air mechanic in the Flying Corps.
I dished out dope, and I swung the prop,
And I polished up my talents in the fitters' shop;
And I did my work so carefully
That now I'm a General at the Ministry.

As an air mechanic I made such a name,
A sergeant-major I soon became,
I wore a tunic and Sam Browne belt,
And my presence on parade was most acutely felt.
My presence was felt so overwhelmingly
That now I'm a general at the Ministry.

As a sergeant-major I made such a hit
That I demanded further scope to do my bit,
Of my lofty ways there was never any doubt
And they sent me up in a Nieuport Scout,
I flew so well over land and sea
That now I'm a General at the Ministry.

I flew in France with such amazing zest
That the King grew tired of adorning my chest,
People boosted McCudden, Bishop and Ball,
But readily agreed that I out-soared them all.
My merits were declared so overwhelmingly
That now I'm a General at the Ministry.
So mechanics all, wherever you be,
If you want to climb to the top of the tree,

If your soul isn't fettered to a pail of dope,
Just take my tip – there's always hope,
Be smart in the Strand at saluting me
And *you'll* be General at the Ministry.

'Nieuport Scout': a RFC aircraft. 'Sam Browne': an officer's waist and shoulder belt. 'McCudden, Bishop and Ball': all famous fighter aces of the RFC. 'Dope': a varnish applied to the cloth surface of aeroplane parts to keep them taut and airtight.

DIRTY DANNY'S DIGGING DEEPER DUG-OUTS

Tune: *'Sister Susie's Sewing Shirts for Soldiers'*

This song was a great favourite of 54 Squadron.

> Dirty Danny's digging deeper dug-outs,
> Much deeper dug-outs dirty Danny dug to make a fug,
> One day he dug a topper,
> But the General came a cropper
> In that damn, deeper, dug-out Danny dug.
>
> Heavy-handed Hans flies Halberstadters,
> In handy Halbertstadters for a flight our Hans does start;
> His Oberst says, 'O dash it,
> For I fear that he will crash it,
> See how heavy-handed Hans ham-handles handy
> Halberstadts!'

'Halberstadt' was the German fighter aircraft Albatros Halberstadt.
'Oberst' is a Colonel.

CANADIAN AND
AMERICAN SONGS

WHEN YOUR BOY COMES BACK TO YOU

A Canadian song, written in 1916 by Gordon V. Thompson and arranged
by Jules Brazil

Keep the lamp of hope still brightly burning,
Till your boy comes back to you;
And although your heart may oft be yearning
For one whose love is true,
Bear in mind the day he'll be returning;
So then, cheer up! Don't be blue!
Ev'ry day you're far apart you grow dearer to his heart,
Till your boy comes back to you!

CHORUS
When your boy comes back to you,
You will keep your promise true;
You will watch, you will wait by the old garden gate,
Till the regiment appears in view
When your boy comes back to you
And the bands are playing too
Won't your heart be beating fast,
Just to welcome him at last?
When your boy comes back to you!

Don't forget to heed this word of warning,
It will mean so much to you;
Though it's dark tonight the sun at morning
Will shine with brighter hue
On the boys with glory all adorning;
You will share that glory too!
Wear a bright and sunny smile,
Tho' you wait a long long while,
Till your boy comes back to you!

ROAMING IN THE TRENCHES

Tune: *'Roamin' in the Gloamin'*

When the Canadian Expeditionary Force (CEF) first went to war, it carried the 'Ross' rifle, which was an excellent target weapon but unsuited to the rigours of military service. Among other faults, the bolt head could be reassembled incorrectly so that it did not lock properly and, on firing, the unlocked bolt was fired back into the firer's head.

The Ross rifle was later replaced by the Lee-Enfield which was used by the British troops.

> Roaming in the trenches, Ross rifle by my side,
> Roaming in the trenches couldn't fire if I tried,
> It's worse than all the rest, the Lee-Enfield I like best,
> I'd like to lose it roaming in the trenches.

TAKE ME BACK TO DEAR OLD CANADA

Tune: *'Take Me Back to Dear Old Blighty'*

The Canadian troops had their own idea of Blighty.

> Take me back to dear old Canada,
> Put me on the boat for old St. John,
> Take me over there, drop me anywhere,
> Toronto, Hull or Montreal, well I don't care.
> I should love to see my best girl,
> Cuddling up again we soon should be, whoa,
> Tiddley, iddley, 'ighty, I'd sooner be there than Blighty,
> Canada is the place for me.

OVER THERE

Lyrics and music by George M. Cohan

For the American soldiers, known as Doughboys, this was their favourite. The song, first sung at the New York Hippodrome for a Red Cross benefit, swept the nation as its Army confidently left their country to fight a war in Europe. However, this somewhat bombastic song didn't go down so well with the British and Colonial Troops – among them the many Americans who were 'honorary Canadians' – having gone to Canada to enlist before America entered the war. The U.S. declared war in April 1917, and sent a token force of two divisions to be attached to the French army. It was 1918 before the Americans began to arrive in force, and May 1918 before they went into action on their own at Cantigny. A more cynical American version of the last line of the chorus substitutes '*And we won't come back, we'll be buried over there.*'

Johnnie, get your gun, get your gun, get your gun,
Take it on the run, on the run, on the run,
Hear them calling you and me, ev'ry son of liberty
Right away, no delay, go today
Make your Daddy glad to have had such a lad,
Tell your sweetheart not to pine, to be proud her boy's in line.

CHORUS
Over there, over there!
Send the word, send the word over there!
That the Yanks are coming, the Yanks are coming,
The drums rum-tumming ev'rywhere!
So prepare, say a prayer,
Send the word, send the word to beware!
We'll be over, we're coming over,
And we won't come back 'til it's over over there.

Johnnie, get your gun, get your gun, get your gun,
Johnnie show the Hun you're a son of a gun!
Hoist the flag and let her fly,
Yankee Doodle do or die
Pack your little kit, show your grit, do your bit
Yankees to the ranks form the towns and the tanks
Make your mother proud of you and the old Red White and Blue.

The British Tommies had a different, sardonic last line to the song!

Over there, over there!
Send the word, send the word, over there!
That the Yanks are coming, the Yanks are coming,
The drums rum-tumming ev'rywhere.
So prepare, say a prayer,
Send the word, send the word to beware!
They're coming over, they're coming over
And they won't get there 'til it's over, *over* there.

HOW'YA GONNA KEEP 'EM DOWN ON THE FARM?

Lyrics by Sam M. Lewis and Joe Young, with music by Walter Donaldson

The idea that American soldiers had any chance of enjoying the delights of 'Paree' is rather comical; nevertheless, the song was extremely popular in America in 1918.

Reuben, Reuben, I've been thinking said his wifey dear
Now that all is peaceful and calm, the boys will soon be back on the farm,
Mister Reuben started winking, and slowly rubbed his chin;
He pulled his chair up close to mother, and he asked her with a grin;

CHORUS
How'ya gonna keep 'em down on the farm, after they've seen Paree?
How'ya gonna keep 'em away from Broadway; Jazzin' a'roun' and paintin' the town?
How'ya gonna keep 'em away from harm? That's a mystery.
They'll never want to see a rake or plow, and who the deuce can parley-vous a cow?
How'ya gonna keep'em down on the farm, after they've seen Paree?

Reuben, Reuben, you're mistaken, said his wifey dear;
Once a farmer always a jay, and farmers always stick to hay;
Mother Reuben, I'm not fakin' tho' you may think it strange;
But wine and women play the mischief, with a boy who's loose with change:

CHORUS
How'ya gonna keep 'em down on the farm, after they've seen Paree?(etc.)

THE LAST LONG MILE

Marching Song; words and music by Emil Breitenfeld

An American version of a song also sung by the Tommies.

Oh they put me in the army and they handed me a pack,
They took away my nice new clothes and dolled me up in kack;
They marched me twenty miles a day to ft me for the war,
I didn't mind the first nineteen but the last one made me sore:

CHORUS
Oh it's not the pack that you carry on your back,
Nor the Springfield on your shoulder,
Nor the five inch crust of France's dirty dust
That makes you feel your limbs are growing older,
And it's not the hike on the hard turnpike,
That wipes away your smile,
Nor the socks of the sisters that raise the blooming blisters,
It's the last long mile.

Some day they'll send us over and they'll put us in a trench,
Takin' pot shots at the Fritzes with the Tommies and the French,
And some day we'll be marching through a town across the
   Rhine,
And then you bet we'll all forget these mournful words of mine:

CHORUS
Oh it's not the pack (etc.)

'Springfield' was a rifle used by American soldiers.
'Kack' is short for khaki.

JOE SOAP'S ARMY

Tune: *'Onward Christian Soldiers'*

'Joe Soap' was the American equivalent of 'Tommy Atkins', i.e. an ordinary soldier.

> Forward Joe Soap's Army,
> Marching without fear,
> With our old Commander
> Safely in the rear,
> He boasts and skites
> From morn to night
> And he thinks he's very brave,
> But the men who really did the job
> Are dead and in their grave.
>
> Forward Joe Soap's Army
> Marching without fear
> With our old Commander
> Safely in the rear.

This version of the song was sung at Liverpool docks by British soldiers on the quayside, when the first Americans arrived; in fact, there was never any conscription in the American Army.

> Onward Yankee soldiers
> Onward as to war
> You would not be conscripts
> Had you come before.

THE ROSE OF NO-MAN'S-LAND

Written in 1918 by J. Caddigan with music by James A. Brennan

This American song, though sentimental, struck a note of truth, and no concert party was complete without a plaintive rendering of the song by a tenor.

I've seen some beautiful flowers
Grow in my garden fair,
I've spent some wonderful hours
Lost in their fragrance rare.
But I have found another
Wondrous beyond compare.

CHORUS:
There's a rose that grows in no-
man's land
And it's wonderful to see,
Tho' it's sprayed with tears
It will live for years
In my garden of memory.
It's the one red rose the soldier knows,
It's the work of the Master's hand;
In the War's great curse,
Stands the Red Cross nurse
She's the rose of no-man's-land.

Out in the heavenly splendour,
Down to trial of woe,
God in his mercy has sent her,
Cheering the world below.
We call her 'Rose of Heaven',
We've learned to love her so.

EPILOGUE

STONY-BROKE IN NO-MAN'S-LAND

Written and composed by Herbert Rule, Fred Holt & George Carney

This post war song, written in 1921, captured the mood of many of the soldiers who on their return from war found that there were no homes fit for heroes. They had survived in the belief that life would be richer for them after the war. Employers were obliged to give returning soldiers their jobs back, but there was nothing to stop them sacking them a few weeks later.

In nineteen fourteen, a hundred years ago it seems,
When first the world was awakened from its peaceful dreams,
The bugle called,
I went away,
They said I was a Man then
Ah, but what am I today?

CHORUS
I can't get the old job, can't get the new,
Can't carry on as I used to do.
I look around me and daily I see,
Thousands and thousands of fellows a lot worse off than me.
In Piccadilly friends pass me by,
I'm absolutely stranded in the Strand.
But I confess, I was contented more or less,
When I was stony-broke in No-Man's-Land.

When I donned khaki, the people praised my attitude,
They said 'My lad, you will earn your country's gratitude'.
I chucked my job, I packed my kit
And now I'm down and out but still,
I'm glad I've done my bit.

CHORUS
I can't get the old job, can't get the new (etc.)

I'm not complaining, I know I'm not the only one,
Whose job was promised back.
That promise came undone,
They cheered us then, their flags displayed
But now we are forgotten like the promises they made.

CHORUS
I can't get the old job, can't get the new (etc.)